All Shall Be Well
An Approach to Wellness

All Shall Be Well

An Approach to Wellness

William S. Craddock, Jr., editor

Church Publishing
NEW YORK

Library of Congress Cataloging-in-Publication Data

Craddock, William S., Jr.
    All shall be well: an approach to wellness
    Edited by William S. Craddock, Jr.

Church Publishing Incorporated
445 Fifth Avenue
New York, NY 10016

www.churchpublishing.org

5 4 3 2 1

Acknowledgments

I am grateful for the work of the many writers who have contributed essays for this book. Their perspectives, insights, and stories have provided us with many views of wellness and offered numerous strategies and hopes for a healthy, wholesome, and meaningful life. I am thankful for Joan Castagnone who served as my senior editor, offering encouragement and assistance and supervising the editing process for this book.

I express my deep gratitude to significant mentors and dear friends who, over the years, have encouraged me to work collaboratively in the development of the CREDO program and its significant focus on wellness: the late John Cannon, former chair of the Church Pension Fund; Alan Blanchard, president emeritus of the Church Pension Fund; the late William Andersen, former executive director of the Episcopal Church Foundation; the Very Reverend James Fenhagen, former dean of General Theological Seminary and spiritual leader of the first CREDO team.

I extend my thanks to Vincent Currie, chair of CREDO Institute, Inc.; the directors and advisors of CREDO Institute, Inc. who have guided the CREDO program over the past ten years; to the senior staff of the Church Pension Fund: Dennis Sullivan, the Rev. Canon Patricia M. Coller, Barton T. Jones, and Daniel A. Kasle; the board of trustees of the Church Pension Fund, who have steadfastly provided financial support of CREDO; to Davis Perkins and the Church Publishing staff; and to all of the CREDO faculty and staff, particularly Debbie Burnette, the Rev. Mike Ehmer, the Rev. Gay Jennings, and Cheryl Henderson.

Table of Contents

Contributors

The Very Rev. Canon Michael J. Battle, Ph.D.
Michael is priest-in-charge of The Church of Our Saviour in San Gabriel, California. Previously, he served as academic dean at Virginia Theological Seminary, assistant professor of spirituality and Black Church studies at Duke University Divinity School, and rector of St. Ambrose Episcopal Church in Raleigh, North Carolina. Michael has taught at the University of the South's School of Theology, has worked as an inner-city chaplain with Tony Campolo Ministries, and overseas in Uganda and Kenya with the Plowshares Institute. For two years (1993 and 1994), Michael lived in residence with Archbishop Desmond Tutu in South Africa, and was ordained a priest by the archbishop. Michael holds certification in spiritual direction from the Shalem Institute, and has received degrees from Duke University, Princeton Theological Seminary, and Yale University.

William S. Craddock, Jr.
After twenty-three years as a business executive, Bill worked with Trinity Church, Wall Street, New York City, in the development and management of The Clergy Leadership Project from 1991 until 1995. For the next five years, he served as director of The Cornerstone Project, a ministry of The Episcopal Church Foundation. Since January of 2001, he has been managing director of CREDO Institute, Inc. Bill has been active in his local parish, Calvary Church in Memphis, and the Diocese of West Tennessee. He has also served as a trustee of The Church Pension Fund and as a board member of The Episcopal Church Foundation.

The Rev. Canon Elizabeth Geitz
Elizabeth is the canon for ministry development and deployment in the Diocese of New Jersey, an award-winning author of seven books, and an editor of *Women's Uncommon Prayers*. She has served as chaplain to national and regional conferences in the Episcopal Church, on the executive committee of the Transition Ministry Conference, and as a parish priest from 1993 to 2000. A graduate of Vanderbilt University, Elizabeth received an M.A.T. from the University of South Carolina and an M.Div. from General Theological Seminary, which awarded her the 2007 Distinguished Alumna Award. She currently serves on the GTS Board of Trustees.

The Rev. Dr. Robert R. Hansel
Bob retired to Sun City, Hilton Head in South Carolina, where he serves as an assisting priest at All Saints Church. In April 2007, he completed a three-year appointment as minister of Chapel By-the-Sea, the century-old interdenominational ministry on Captiva Island in southwest Florida. In 2004, he completed a two-year interim assignment at Calvary Episcopal Church in Memphis, Tennessee. In addition to parish ministry, Bob has been a prison chaplain, national church staff member, headmaster of a church-related boarding school, conference center program director, congregational development consultant, and interim and diocesan canon to the ordinary. An earned doctorate has made him appreciate the importance of disciplined study, and overseas stints have helped him gain a global perspective.

The Rev. Canon Scott Hayashi
Currently, Scott is the canon to the ordinary in the Diocese of Chicago. He previously served in dioceses in Spokane, Utah, and California as a vicar or rector of congregations in rural, inner-city, and suburban settings. Scott has worked on various projects for the Episcopal Church, both on the diocesan and national level. He is a graduate of the Harvard Divinity School and was ordained in 1984.

Elaine Hollensbe, Ph.D.
Elaine is a faculty member in the College of Business at the University of Cincinnati, where she also directs the management department's doctoral program and teaches team dynamics, organizational behavior, and human resource management. She has published both quantitative (goal setting, compensation, and self-efficacy) and qualitative (identity, fairness, work-home balance, and emotion) research in top journals in the management field. She has worked with the CREDO Institute, the College for Bishops, and Fresh Start as an evaluation consultant. She lives in Cincinnati and enjoys visiting her two sons in Tennessee and Colorado.

The Rt. Rev. Mark Hollingsworth, Jr.
Mark has been the bishop of the Diocese of Ohio since 2004. He was Archdeacon in the Diocese of Massachusetts from 1995 to 2004 and served as rector, associate rector, and chaplain in numerous churches and schools in the past. He is currently on the Board of Trustees for Church Divinity School of the Pacific, Kenyon College, Episcopal Preaching Foundation, and the Ocean Classroom Foundation. Mark has also served as a Conference Leader on the CREDO faculty and been a member of the Advisory Committee of CREDO Institute, Inc. He received his B.A. from Trinity College, Hartford Connecticut and his M. Div. from Church Divinity School of the Pacific.

The Most Rev. Dr. Katherine Jefferts Schori
Katherine is the presiding bishop of the Episcopal Church.

Barton T. Jones, Esq.
Bart has been the Senior Vice President, General Counsel and Secretary of the Church Pension Fund since 1999. Prior to that, he was a partner in New York law firms, and he has been a member of the New York State Bar since 1972. He is a member of Grace Church in New York City and is the Treasurer and a Board member of the House of the Redeemer. He is treasurer of the Relief of Widows and Children of Clergymen of the Protestant Episcopal Church in the State of New York and President and Board member of the Williams Club in New York. He received his B.A. in Economics from Williams College and his J.D. from Vanderbilt University School of Law.

Glen E. Kreiner, Ph.D.
Glen is a faculty member at the Smeal College of Business at The Pennsylvania State University, where he teaches organizational behavior and team dynamics. He received his Ph.D. in business administration from Arizona State University and a B.A. in communications and a master's of organizational behavior from Brigham Young University. He has published his research in book chapters and several of his field's top journals. He is currently conducting research on positive identities, temporary workers, and the social and systemic factors involved in the recent global

financial crisis. He has been involved in two major research projects involving the Episcopal Church ("Borders and Bridges" and "The Episcopal Identity Project"). He lives with his wife and three children in central Pennsylvania, where they all enjoy gardening together.

The Rt. Rev. Jeffrey D. Lee
Jeffrey D. Lee was elected the 12th bishop of the Diocese of Chicago on November 10, 2007, and consecrated bishop on February 2, 2008. A graduate of Nashotah House Seminary, he was ordained a priest in the Diocese of Northern Indiana in 1985 and has served the church in various capacities including canon to the ordinary for the Diocese of Northern Indiana, rector of St. Christopher's Episcopal Church in River Hills, Wisconsin, and rector of St. Thomas Episcopal Church in Medina, Washington. Lee is the author of *Opening the Prayer Book* in the New Church's Teaching Series; and a contributing author of the Clergy Wellness Report published by the CREDO Institute, and of *The Rite Stuff*, published by Church Publishing. He has served on the faculty of CREDO Institute; and on the boards of the North American Association of the Diaconate, the Council of Associated Parishes, and Affirming Catholicism. He is an associate of the Society of St. John the Evangelist.

The Rev. Canon Hartshorn Murphy, Jr.
Since 1997, Hartshorn has served as senior pastor of St. Augustine by-the-Sea Episcopal Church in Santa Monica, California. He has pastored churches in Baltimore, Milwaukee, and South Central Los Angeles. Prior to his present position, Hartshorn served the Bishop of Los Angeles as executive for mission and congregational development. He graduated with a B.A. in philosophy from the University of Maryland and an M.Div. from Virginia Theological Seminary.

The Rev. Canon M. Renée Miller
Renée serves as priest for St. Andrew's in Marianna, Arkansas. In addition to her role as senior editor and project manager for explorefaith.org, she owns two businesses in Memphis, Tennessee. Renée served as canon to the ordinary and deployment officer for the Diocese of Idaho from 1988 to 1997 and for the Diocese of El Camino Real from 1997 to 2001. Renée is a graduate of Northeastern Illinois University and Seabury-Western Theological Seminary.

The Rev. Dr. Sam Portaro
Ordained in 1975, Sam served as vicar at Church of the Epiphany in Newton, North Carolina; as an Episcopal chaplain to the College of William and Mary in Virginia; and associate to the rector of Bruton Parish Church in Williamsburg, Virginia. Sam retired in December 2004 after twenty-two years of service as the Episcopal chaplain at the University of Chicago. He is the author of seven books and continues his ministry of writing, speaking, retreat direction, and consulting. Sam is a graduate of UNC-Chapel Hill and Virginia Theological Seminary. He earned his D.Min. from Princeton Theological Seminary.

Mathew L. Sheep, Ph.D.
Mathew teaches organizational behavior and leadership at Illinois State University, having received his Ph.D. in business administration and a master's degree in communication from the University of Cincinnati. Mathew's research is published in top

journals such as the *Academy of Management Journal, Human Relations*, and the *Journal of Business Ethics*. Mathew is involved in research projects for the CREDO Institute, Inc. and College for Bishops. Prior to his current academic career, Mathew served as a commissioned officer in the United States Coast Guard and as a senior minister in the Christian Church. Mathew lives with his wife, Barbara, and daughter, Melissa, in Bloomington, Illinois, and enjoys running and electronic music creation as his hobbies.

The Rev. Joseph A. Stewart-Sicking, Ed.D.

Joe is an Assistant Professor of Pastoral Counseling and Spiritual Care at Loyola University Maryland. From 2003–2006, he was the Program Associate for the Project on Congregations of Intentional Practice at Virginia Theological Seminary, a national study examining how traditional Christian practices are related to congregational vitality. He has also served as a mental health counselor in hospital, prison, addictions, and congregational settings. He earned his B.S. in Physics from Xavier University and his Ed.D. in counselor education and supervision from University of Cincinnati. After completing his seminary studies at Virginia Theological Seminary, he was ordained a priest in 2008 and serves as a Chaplain at Washington National Cathedral among other assignments.

Phyllis T. Strupp

Phyllis is a brain-fitness mentor and author, and a leader of the Episcopal Ecological Network and the Diocese of Arizona's Nature and Spirituality Program. From 1988–2007, she worked as a financial representative with Northwestern Mutual, specializing in insurance and benefit products. From 1982 until 1988 she held financial management positions at Dun & Bradstreet and Equitable Life in New York. An EFM mentor from 2000–2007, Phyllis earned a B.A. in history from Rutgers University, an M.B.A. in finance from Columbia University, and CLU/CHFC designations from the American College.

The Rev. Brian C. Taylor

Brian has been the rector of St. Michael and All Angels in Albuquerque, New Mexico, since 1983. He is the author of several books on spirituality and prayer, a retreat leader, spiritual director, and teacher of contemplative prayer. A native of the San Francisco Bay area, Brian attended college in Vermont, went to seminary at the Church Divinity School of the Pacific, and served his first two years of ordained ministry at Grace Cathedral in San Francisco. He is a guitarist and enjoys creating fresh expressions of traditional liturgical patterns.

The Rev. Dr. William J. Watson, III

Bill was ordained in 2003 and is the rector of Grace Church in Hopkinsville, Kentucky. He is particularly interested in family systems theory and encouraging healthy lifestyles. Bill also volunteers as a family physician at St. Luke Free Clinic. He has served on Trustees and Council, the Standing Committee, and the Commission on Ministry in the Diocese of Kentucky. Bill earned a B.A. and M.Ed. (health education) from the University of Virginia. In 1979, he earned an M.D. from Eastern Virginia Medical School, and practiced family medicine in Newport News, Virginia, until 2000. He earned his M.Div. in 2003 from Virginia Theological Seminary.

Foreword—All Shall Be Well

Katherine Jefferts Schori

Julian of Norwich is famous for the assurance she heard in a time of great distress, "all shall be well, all shall be well, and all manner of thing shall be well." It was a message like that of each angelic messenger of the Bible, "fear not." It is most essentially a statement of confidence in the vision God has for us all, that we and our relationships are ultimately to be healed. That work of healing and wholeness is an integral part of leadership in the Church, for it is a healing savior we proclaim, who challenged his followers to "heal, and proclaim that the Reign of God has come near." Wholeness, holiness, and health are part of the divine dream for creation.

The work of CREDO is meant to equip leaders in the Church to attend to their own healing and wholeness in every sphere of existence, that they may in turn lead others into greater health. You will encounter here a focus on a recurrent movement toward greater health of all sorts, in the shorthand of *identity, discernment, practice,* and *transformation.* This is a framework for the work of Christian discipleship as a leader, and it is a model that can be taught and learned. Beginning to look at one's own identity as a creature, and as a member of interdependent communities, can empower the leader to challenge other systems to attend in similar ways to the possibilities of transformation.

Jesus has invited us into this work of transformation, on behalf of the world. We are all leaders by virtue of baptism. Come exploring, and re-discover how *all shall be well* in your own life and the life of the larger world.

1

Introduction

William S. Craddock, Jr.

All shall be well
and all shall be well
and all manner of things shall be well.

—Julian of Norwich, 1342–1416

Julian of Norwich, whose childhood was scarred by the famine, poverty, peasant revolts, and the black plague that swept across Europe, left an enduring legacy to future generations, which can be captured with these simple words of steadfast and unfailing hope. At the age of thirty, suffering from a severe illness and believing she was on her deathbed, Julian had a series of intense visions that she recorded. Twenty years later, they became the source of her major work, *Sixteen Revelations of Divine Love.* Julian's theology was optimistic, positive, and hope-filled—a solid sign of her own wellness, wholeness, and holiness.

I remember one early September morning in 1993, mist rising over the fields, as I walked along a gravel road with a friend in anticipation of my first trout fly-fishing experience. I had the right outfit—waders, fishing vest, long-billed hat, Polaroid sunglasses, and a little box of flies. The previous day, I had received tedious, explicit instructions about how to tie the fly on a tippet, the tiny monofilament line at the end of a fly-line leader. I had learned how to synchronize bending my elbow and moving my forearm and wrist like a metronome to cast a .002 ounce fly to within inches of a swirling spot in the river. I was all set and focused with mounting anticipation as I waded into the cool, clear stream and spotted my first trout hovering in the current. Pulling out the fly line to begin my repetitive casts, I had a distinct feeling of being well—all was right with the world and me.

But, then it all began to unravel—literally! Even before I completed my first cast, my line had been transformed into a tangled mouse nest. My exuberant mood suddenly gave way to irritation, frustration, and a sinking feeling as I stared down at the mess of line hanging limply over my waders. My immediate impulse was to pull out my knife and cut out the knots. But after some not-so-quiet and then some very quiet dialogue with myself, I began to realize that I was also reflecting inwardly on the tangled knots in my own life. Staring at the rippling currents in the river as it moved swiftly downstream—always toward the ocean—I contemplated the calming rhythm, coupling continuity and change that always looks the same. As Heraclitus said, "You cannot step twice into the same river." The river reflected my interior life—a dance of continuity and change. For a long time, I was unaware of the depth and complexity of my experience. Not only did I not have the answers, I didn't even have the questions.

I folded the knife and put it back in my pocket. Slowly and patiently, I began to untangle the loops and knots in the line thinking about the stresses, fears, and concerns of my life and how they have often overshadowed my feelings of gratitude, joy, and my sense of well-being. I began to reflect on what techniques, what practices, what resources would be helpful in providing me with a more positive, healthy outlook on my life.

Over the past ten years or so, I have been privileged and blessed to participate in a broad culture of wellness in the Episcopal Church called CREDO. This initiative is a benefit for clergy and lay participants in the Church Pension Fund and provides an opportunity for them to examine significant areas of life and then, with the support of a Christ-centered community, invites participants to go deep inside themselves to rediscover this place of peace, wellness, wholeness, and holiness. It is in these blessed moments of transformation that CREDO participants can realize God's presence in their soul and move forward in their vocation with renewed energy, passion, and the resolve to live authentically as one with God through Christ.

The primary purpose of this book is to introduce a comprehensive approach to wellness and offer opportunities for readers to reflect on their own lives and their sense of well-being through various insights, and perspectives. The core model offered in this book tracks four developmental phases of self-awareness: identity, discernment, practice, and transformation. Each chapter will explore this developmental process with contributions from a gifted specialist. The writers come from a variety of disciplines and offer their stories and their insights into the broad topics of self-development and wellness. These insights will, I hope, challenge readers to integrate the many dimensions of their lives and become more aware of their capacity not only to learn how to be, but also to practice being, to live fully into a life of health, energy, and vitality with increased confidence and conviction to discern God's calling.

Models and theories are imperfect representations of reality, but they can assist the seeker to refresh and/or revise his or her concepts and understandings of identity and relationships. A common strategic-thinking model used in the business world is centered on three phases: Where am I? Where am I going? How am I going to get there? Although this is a practical and useful approach, I believe there is something missing in this method—God!

The fundamental model outlined in this book is centered on four phases and their respective questions:

1. Identity—Who am I?

2. Discernment—Who is God calling me to be?

3. Practice—How am I responding to God's call?

4. Transformation—How am I changing?

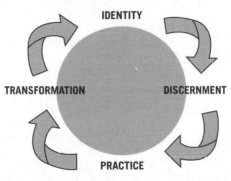

Upon answering the last question "How am I changing?" one realizes that integrating these sequential phases results in an ongoing cyclical pattern—with the last question, the process begins anew—spiraling upwards with greater understanding and awareness of one's progressing self. As T.S. Eliot beautifully phrased it:

And the end of all our exploring
Will be to arrive where we started
And to know the place for the first time.

Understanding and applying this dynamic feedback loop may guide us into a keen awareness of a blessed life of health, wholeness, and holiness.

Wellness, or well-being, is difficult to define. The specifics of wellness vary from individual to individual and from situation to situation. It may mean engaging in one set of behaviors at one time and in very different behaviors at another time. One universal defining mark of wellness is flexibility and adaptability in both the personal and professional areas of life. Wellness also involves the willingness to know one's self, and it involves the ability to be aware of our capacity to function so as to enhance our life and the lives of those around us.

Wellness includes having a clear set of core values. It includes our ability to discern our vocation, channel our passions, set goals, and achieve them or at least work towards them. It means having the capacity to initiate, sustain, and deepen relationships. Wellness is reflected in our experiences of satisfaction and fulfillment in many areas of life—personal, family, and professional.

All of these dimensions can arguably be tied to a pervasive and comprehensive sense of wellness, but the vital relationship, the unseen force and mover of our well-being, is our relationship with God.

Tao says:

> We join spokes together in a wheel
> But it is the center hole
> That makes the wagon move.

As the center of our life, God calls us to an abundant life—not a life without stress or challenge—but a life that meets those challenges and stresses in a way that draws upon the resources of our faith in communion and community with others. This is the foundation for a comprehensive approach to wellness.

IDENTITY
Who Am I?

Life is to be lived forward but it is understood backward.

—Søren Kierkegaard

Identity is an umbrella term usually used to describe an individual's comprehension of self as a discrete, separate entity. Identity is, simply, a sense of self that remains constant and identifiable across a variety of situations and circumstances. The essays in this chapter introduce a more relational understanding of identity—connecting and balancing the concept of the individual with others and with God. This broader perspective of identity may lead us to a richer sense of wellness, wholeness, and holiness in our lives.

Based on their work for the CREDO "Borders and Bridges" research project, Drs. Kreiner, Hollensbe, and Sheep introduce practical social science concepts about identity in their essay, "Balancing the 'Me' and the 'We.'" They suggest that the tension between the need to be unique and the need to belong is a life-long balancing act along the path to wellness.

In "Toward a Theology of Wellness," the Rt. Rev. Jeffrey Lee ties the concept of wellness with identity. He shares a personal glimpse of his relationship with his son to convey the essence of loving and being loved by God.

In "Values to Live By," the Rev. Dr. Robert R. Hansel explores identity through a foundational awareness of our core values. Robert refers to values as standards, used as a compass, helping people steer a life-course that is responsible and meaningful. He suggests a set of Christian core values that underlie and sustain us in our lives.

The Very Rev. Canon Michael J. Battle, Ph.D. addresses the murky waters of identity with Ubuntu, an African spirituality that begins with community and moves to individuality. In his essay, "Toward a Theology of Identity," Michael invites us to rethink our modern, isolated, Cartesian sense of identity and begin to understand a more relational ontology, an identity interdependent with others as expressed in the powerful aphorism: "I am because we are."

Dr. Mathew L. Sheep, a researcher and assistant professor at Illinois State University, examines the relationship of identity to wellness along three dimensions: multiplicity, different levels, and change. Throughout his essay, "The Relationships of Identity to wellness," Mathew emphasizes ways that individuals, as people of God, can more clearly know themselves, their connections with others, and the critical role of health and wellness in navigating change and serving others.

Balancing the "Me" and the "We"

Identity Work as a Path toward Wellness[1]

Glen E. Kreiner
Elaine C. Hollensbe
Mathew L. Sheep

*I think a lot of clergy take themselves way too seriously.
My metaphor is that they need to buy a collar that is
one-half inch bigger because the one they are wearing
is way too tight, and cuts off oxygen to their brain.*

—Episcopal priest

Have you ever felt like your job, your family, or some other obligation is completely defining you? Have you ever wondered where the unique "you" disappeared amidst all the demands on your time, talent, and energies? You're not alone. In addition to your own experiences, you can probably pretty easily think of a friend, a family member, or a neighbor who seems to be working too hard, losing themselves to work or social obligations, or just generally too spent for healthy living. Why is this happening? And what can we do about it—for ourselves and for those around us?

This chapter is about the search for "optimal balance"—the "just right" equilibrium between being ourselves and being what other people want us to be. In the chapter, we share some insights as to why this might be happening. We hope that we can provide a language for understanding some of these challenges, with the hope that the language can give you power over the problem.

Let's start with what research has shown to be a universal challenge—that every individual lives in a constant tension between two aspects of self—the *social* identity, which comes from group memberships such as roles, occupation, or church, and the *personal* identity, which represents the aspects of self that are unique to each person, areas such as personal history or personality profile. When we rely too much on the social aspects of identity (our jobs or social connections), we lose our sense of self as a unique human being. The "me" gets lost in the "we." On the other hand, when we rely too much on the personal aspects of identity, we are cut off from others. The "me" loses a healthy connection to the "we." We find that, perhaps paradoxically, by acknowledging our limits as human beings, we empower ourselves to be better instruments for good. In fact, Jesus found it necessary to withdraw from others at times—to seek solitude and achieve balance by being alone in prayer—perhaps to renew a clear sense of his identity and mission: "Jesus often withdrew to lonely places and prayed." (Luke 5:15–16)

Of course, each of us differs in our approaches to balancing the "we" and the "me." Research has demonstrated that individuals vary in how much they want to manifest their unique identities as opposed to defining themselves in terms of a collective. It is worthwhile to pause and ask yourself the following questions:

What parts of me are defined by the groups to which I belong?

Am I satisfied with how and how much they define me?

Do I need more individuality in the way I see myself, or do I need more of a sense of belonging?

As we ponder these questions, we help ourselves to recognize the need for change. We call moving toward this change "identity work."

Identity Work

Identity work is what people can do to create and sustain a healthy sense of self. Individuals engage in identity work as they struggle to find and maintain the optimal balance between the "me" and the "we." In our work with Episcopal clergy, we found three major ways that individuals can undertake identity work: through *segmenting* tactics, *integrating* tactics, and *dual-role* or *neutral* tactics.[2]

Segmenting Tactics

People can use segmenting tactics in identity work to differentiate their personal identity (me) from their social identity (we). We documented several ways people can segment, limit, prioritize, and relegate social identities to carve out space for personal identity. This process helps crystallize the "me" among the demands of the "we."

Separating Role from Identity

With this tactic, an individual is able to separate the "what I do" from the "who I am." Distinguishing between doing and being helps to gain control over identity-shaping processes instead of being consumed by them. One cleric described the priesthood in this way:

> I feel like it is all of my being. I can't just discard it. It's [like] a cloth that has been soaked with a stain that is through and through— and yet I am constantly aware of [other] roles. So, when I'm here at work, I am 100% conscious that I am a priest and I'm acting as a priest. When I am home, I am constantly shifting gears and saying, "Now I'm a wife and a mother." Although the priest part of me pops up every now and then, and I'm aware of it. When I'm with friends or whatever, I have to consciously tell myself, "You are being a friend.". . . I see myself as 24/7 and thoroughly soaked with my priestly call and identity and all that [but] I'm also conscious of when I'm operating in which role.

As this statement demonstrates, the effort to separate identity ("Who am I?") from the various roles in which one engages ("What do I do?") can be quite intentional. Another segmentation tactic is to set limits on how much we allow social identities to consume us.

Setting Limits

Sometimes, demands from home or work infringe on us to such a degree that we begin to feel that our boundaries have collapsed. Yet, by acknowledging our limits as human beings, we empower ourselves. First, we recognize the temporal and physical restraints upon ourselves, particularly in identity-demanding occupations such as the priesthood. Second, we can set more realistic expectations about who we are and what is within the scope of our responsibilities and abilities. The adage "don't let the perfect be the enemy of the good" can be applied to our own follies in pursuing perfection—such quests are not only unrealistic, they can tear down our self-concept and take our eyes off the target of continuous improvement.

Creating an Identity Hierarchy

Of course, not every demand in our lives gets the same amount of attention. Individuals can create a hierarchy—a pecking order of sorts—among their identity demands. Creating a hierarchy empowers the individual by creating order out of perceived chaos, and provides a rubric for in-the-moment decision making. Also, creating the hierarchy helps to clarify roles as separate from our core selves, further separating the "me" and "we." Several of the identity aspects in our research include: priest, child of God, parent, spouse, community activist, and Christian. We also noted that placing something other than the priesthood first further aided in creating a differentiation between self and vocation. As one priest explained, "I think that becoming a mother, that is what my identity is. Even more strongly so than being a priest." As we improve our ability to prioritize identity demands, we not only empower ourselves, but we also can obtain a healthier overall self-concept.

Enacting Ephemeral Roles

Another way to differentiate self from a strong social identity is to take a break from that identity and immerse yourself in a temporary or ephemeral role. This could be a one-time experiment or an ongoing escape that allows you to leave the social identity behind (either fully or partially) and enter into a very different role. For example, one priest said, "You need places where you can step out of that role as a priest." We found a wide range of ephemeral roles, including athlete (joining a kayaking club, bicycling), musician (composing music, joining bands), artist (painting, writing), and social group member (joining environmentalist groups, creating informal clubs) ones. These pursuits allow us to remove ourselves from the customary demands and see ourselves in new ways.

Integrating Tactics

Individuals can also engage in identity work to integrate their personal and social identities, merging the "me" and "we." For individuals using these tactics, segmentation between personal and social identities becomes less of a concern because overlap of identities is seen as acceptable and even desirable. Examples of such tactics include "merging role with identity," "infusing self-aspects into tasks," and "casting self as emblem." These tactics are explained in the following sections.

Merging Role with Identity

Above, we explained the tactic of separating role (what you do) from identity (who you are) as a segmentation tactic. We also found the reverse process being used in order to more fully integrate oneself with the role. This tactic involves treating the social identity and the role as the same. In terms of the priesthood, this often stemmed from a belief that the priesthood changes your very essence (ontological change). Seeing role and identity as the same allows for a greater integration of that role into your life. As one priest put it:

> It's just part and parcel of every cell in my body. I'm a dad. I'm a husband. I'm an outdoorsman. I'm a priest. It's just a character issue, identity issue. It all goes together. I can't imagine not being one. . . . You are a priest whether you have your collar on or not. You are a priest while you are being a dad. You are a priest while you are being a husband. You are a priest. So, integrate. Learn how to do all that, together.

Infusing Self-Aspects into Tasks

Rather than totally merging role and identity, some individuals strategically integrate particular aspects of their own personal identity into the priesthood role. This often involves a person identifying his or her unique strengths, abilities, and personality dimensions and deciding how to put those dimensions to work in the role. As one clergy member put it, "How I live out the vocation emerges out of who I am. . . . For the most part I feel I bring myself to the task. So how I am a priest emerges out of who I am." Several clergy whom we interviewed in our research gave examples of life experiences (divorce, abuse, past jobs, marital problems, etc.) that they would import into their approach of being a priest (generally) and/or into their relationships with parishioners or other clergy (specifically). This tactic allows for personalization of the role, bringing more of the self into work.

Casting Self as Emblem

The third way individuals integrate social and personal identities is by casting themselves as an emblem (representation) or role model of the identity. This involves framing oneself not as a mere member of the group, but as the very embodiment of it. As one priest told us:

I'm bringing people something that is so much larger than me, than I am. I'm bringing them all the two thousand years of Christian tradition and the comfort of the church and the sacraments and Holy Scripture . . . How I feel about it is completely irrelevant. Yeah, I do think I disappear, but in a kind of paradoxical way, I become more fully authentic. So it is very much who I am, but I just don't matter anymore.

Dual-role/Neutral Tactics

The third categorization of tactics can serve to either integrate *or* segment the "me" and "we," depending on the needs of the individual. These tactics include seeking refreshment, involving other people, and tapping spiritual resources.

Seeking Refreshment

This tactic involves recharging one's identity batteries by removing oneself from the daily demands of the role. A recurring theme in our interviews was the usefulness of some time away. This can range from longer-term and highly structured forms of refreshment (such as a sabbatical) to shorter-term and/or spontaneous forms of rejuvenation (such as finding a quiet place for meditation). For example, the CREDO conferences offered by CREDO Institute offer clergy and lay leaders an opportunity to detach from their regular commitments for several days, reflect on their lives, and rejuvenate themselves. Many of the clergy we interviewed also pointed to the principle of the Sabbath as a guide; as one put it:

Keep a day off. God took a day off once a week. I've heard clergy say things like, "When I work on my day off, I'm giving God two gifts: I'm giving him my work plus my day off. . . ." It makes me sick. I tell them that. I warn young clergy that you know there is a commandment, keep the Sabbath day holy. It is a commandment; it's not a suggestion. . . .

In terms of keeping the Sabbath holy, it's not just going to church on Sunday, it's taking a twenty-four hour period to rest. . . . [Clergy need] to have in their lives as a habit a near sacrosanct day of the week that everybody knows. It's not like, "Oh, poor guy needs a rest." It's more like, "This is part of my worship. This is the way I serve God and you can and should, too."

Involving Other People

Clearly, identity demands are driven in large part by the pressures and expectations put on us by other people. The inherently relational nature of identity can be used to our advantage as well. We noted how some clergy were able to involve other people strategically to help with their identity work. One way to do this is by surrounding oneself with supportive people—staff members, friends, colleagues—who help create ideal conditions for doing identity work as well as engaging in identity work themselves. Another way of involving other people is to target specific individuals or groups who can help. In our research, this included family members (e.g., a spouse being a good check against workaholism), support groups (e.g., "colleague groups" composed of other clergy), and finding friends who were completely disassociated from the church and/ or parish (in order to have friendships not tied to the priesthood).

Tapping Spiritual Resources

Perhaps ironically for a study of clergy, several noted that they had to work particularly hard to maintain their own spirituality, and that it could easily go undeveloped. One told us, "Some clergy don't rely on God. They try to rely on their own inner resources. You can get burned out there. You need to care for your own spiritual life." Clergy we interviewed mentioned several specific spiritual practices that were linked to their identity work, including prayer, meditation, reading scripture, formal worship services, and guided spiritual direction. Consider how you might pursue issues of identity development as a spiritual path—how might spirit and identity be linked for you and those around you?

Conclusions

All individuals have challenges stemming from the tension between the need to be unique and the need to belong. This is a lifelong balancing act along the path to wellness. As you reflect upon your own current situation, where are you in the balance? Consider how the identity work tactics outlined above might be applied in your own life to your advantage. How might you employ some of these tactics to develop a greater sense of the "me" while still being a viable and vibrant part of the "we?" How might you utilize the intellectual, emotional, spiritual, and human resources available to you on your path to wellness? And how might you help those around you—congregational members, family members, others—as you travel on this path together?

In conjunction with the CREDO Institute, we are on an ongoing journey to better understand how people can negotiate the pressures of identity more effectively. We continue to develop ideas and training materials that can help people better negotiate these demands at work, at home, and at church. We'd love to hear your success stories and suggestions for others, and any other general comments at bordersandbridges@gmail.com. Drop us a note!

☙❧

Notes

1. This chapter is based on our work on the "Borders and Bridges" research project, funded in part by the CREDO Institute, Inc. and on our 2006 publication: G.E. Kreiner, E.C. Hollensbe, M.L. Sheep. "Where is the 'Me' Among the 'We'?: Identity Work and the Search for Optimal Balance," *Academy of Management Journal, 49:* 1031–1057. For this project we interviewed sixty Episcopal priests and analyzed open-ended survey data from another 220 priests.

2. Our data come from clergy; however, lay church leaders, church members, and the general public have found tremendous utility in applying these principles.

Toward a Theology of Wellness
Jeffrey D. Lee

A young boy runs back and forth, up and down the length of a room with soft padding underfoot. He is clearly agitated and sits down suddenly and begins to rock back and forth, hugging his knees. A young man comes up to him, sits down beside him and, hugging his knees, begins to rock just like the boy. They keep this up for a few moments until the boy gives a sideways glance toward the man who is moving just like he is. They establish eye contact, the first person-to-person contact this young boy with autism has made with anyone in a very long time.

I saw this scene last year during a screening of a remarkable film titled, *Autism: The Musical*. Elaine Hill, whose son is the boy in this scene, discovered that while therapists and physicians had failed to make much progress in helping her son to communicate and function in the world, the actors with whom she worked as a director, could and did make a big difference. "Other people tried to force him to respond and act in 'normal' ways," she said. "But actors aren't afraid to act strange—they do it all the time. Instead of expecting my son to get how to function normally they joined his world first and built a bridge to ours." Elaine Hill received a vision from her experience. She gathered a group of kids living with issues all along the autism spectrum, and she worked with them to write, produce, and perform a full-blown musical. The film is a chronicle of their triumph—kids who barely speak or know how to interact with others are able to sing and dance and imagine whole new worlds.

Autism results when the brain receives too much sensory material, too much information. The mind panics and tries to regain control. One way of doing this is to close up the self and do nothing but engage in repeated actions that are familiar, acknowledging no new external stimuli. But if another person can join in the repetitious behavior, there is a chance that the anxious mind of the autistic person might recognize a link with the outside world that is less frightening or as dangerous than it appeared to be.

This is a mirror, a true image of what Christians have to say about healing. The Christian gospel is about the healing of humankind's ancient woundedness, our persistent and tragically self-destructive behavior.[1] We

17

close in on ourselves. We are afraid. The world overwhelms us and so in a million and one inventive ways we shut each other out, we lash out from our anxiety and fearfulness. We hurt ourselves. The Christian tradition calls this alienation and isolation "the fall." It is the story of Adam and Eve, who were originally at one with creation, who knew and delighted in their status as creatures until they were compelled to hide from God and from one another. They lost their capacity to speak to God. And almost immediately their children began to behave in murderous ways. Sin and death have come into the world. But in Christ, God enters our human condition, God joins us, God builds a bridge so that we might know once again whole and holy relationships, with one another and with God. God restores us to health.

Wellness and the Reign of God

The concept of wellness lies very close to the heart of the Gospel. The word salvation itself is closely related to the Latin word for health. Jesus said he came so that we might have abundant life. He tells his friends that they must be whole, wholesome, and complete, just as God is: "Be perfect, just as your heavenly Father is perfect." (Matthew 5:48) The Greek word for perfect is *teleios*, which means to be brought to completion, to maturity, to wholeness. Perhaps the most significant sign of Jesus' identity and his inauguration of the Reign of God was his ministry of healing. Story after story in the Gospels tells us about Jesus' compassion for those who are sick or suffering. When the disciples of John the Baptist ask Jesus if he is the one they have been waiting for, he tells them to go and tell John what they have seen: the blind see, the lame walk, and the poor finally hear the good news. Even the forgiveness of sin is presented in terms of healing and restoration to a state of wellness. The woman caught in the act of adultery is set free from the judgment of her accusers and told to go and sin no more. Jesus restores the integrity of her personhood when he restores her to the community. He makes her well.

The early church continued to understand its experience of the Risen Christ in terms of health and wellness. Immediately after the experience of Pentecost, Peter and John encounter a man lame from birth and tell him all they have to give him is healing in the name of Jesus. The man walks. In some of the earliest writings of the Christian scriptures, Paul pictures the church as the Body of Christ, various parts working together with ease and suppleness so that the whole body might move and grow into maturity. When one member is unhealthy or diseased the whole body suffers. Life in Christ is growth into the image and likeness of Christ who is the perfect image of God. The startling claim of scripture is that the fullness of who God is dwells bodily in Christ and that we come to that same fullness of life because we are members of Christ. (Colossians 2:9–10) To be in union with Christ is to be made well in an ultimate sense.

Wellness results in right relationships, the practice of communion and community.

In the first chapter of the Letter to the Galatians, Paul draws out the purpose of this union with Christ. He says, "God . . . was pleased to reveal his Son in me, so that I might proclaim him among the Gentiles." (Galatians 1:15–16)

The healing and wholeness that comes from God is nothing less than the manifestation of the Risen Christ in the believer. Christ is revealed in us for the purpose of mission, so that God's wholeness and healing love, known and experienced in Jesus, might be extended to the whole world. And that love bears wounds, just as the Risen Jesus showed to Thomas. Even in our obvious weakness and brokenness, we are called to complete reliance on Christ who is revealed in us and through us for the sake of the world. Wellness, in Christian terms, does not mean the absence of weakness or pain. After Paul prayed repeatedly to be relieved of some persistent ailment, the answer he received from God was: "My grace is sufficient for you, for power is made perfect in weakness." (II Corinthians 12:9) God's glory is revealed in the vulnerability and brokenness of Christ in the great mystery of the cross, and every Christian is invited to take up the cross and carry it with and for those who have no choice about bearing it. The wholeness God wills for us has to do with the transformation of our weakness into the love of God for all who suffer. Our wholeness is made complete in compassion.

Theosis—Ultimately Well?

In the Christian tradition, what does it mean to be ultimately well? During its first several centuries, the church developed a rich theological notion called *theosis*, or deification. It can be summarized simply: "God became human, so that humankind might become God." For the early church, this is the essence of salvation. In the seventh century Maximus the Confessor wrote, "Because God has become man, man can become God.

He rises by divine steps corresponding to those by which God humbled himself out of love for men, taking on himself, without any change in himself, the worst of our condition."[2] By our adoption into the Body of Christ, we have access to the perfect life of God. Irenaeus of Lyons says simply, "God is himself the life of those who participate in him."[3] Our humanity is not obliterated by this union with God, but fulfilled. At the deepest level, our identity depends on our relationship with God.

Theologians of the patristic period describe the Christian life as a process of deification in Holy Baptism; body, mind, and spirit are infused with the power and presence of the Holy Spirit and drawn progressively deeper into the eternal reality of God. For the baptized, resurrection begins now. Every Eucharist is an experience of remembering the Body of Christ, a foretaste of the heavenly banquet. A second-century writer called the Eucharist the *pharmakon*, the medicine of immortality.[4] Because we have already begun to taste resurrected life, we are empowered to join together in making the Reign of God a reality in this world. The Holy Spirit draws us into God's project of healing the world. And while this healing work invites our conscious participation, it does not depend on our efforts. Holiness is not a matter of our achieving moral excellence or theological correctness; it is a matter of being grasped by the Spirit of God. We "press on" with the ministry of healing and reconciliation in this world, because Christ has already begun this work in us and in the whole of creation. (Philippians 3:12) This is the mission of the church, to cooperate in God's agenda of mending creation.

Balance and Holy Relationship

Many physicians and other healthcare professionals describe a healthy body as one in which physical systems are in balance, working together with ease so that a person is able to meet the challenges of growth and change and able to engage in life-giving relationships. Similarly, for members of the Body of Christ, the image of the Holy Trinity itself illustrates this dimension of what we mean by wellness. Think of the great classical icon of the Holy Trinity, an image given its most popular form in the fifteenth century by Anton Rublev, a Russian icon maker.

In this image, based on a story in the eighteenth chapter of Genesis in which Christians have long seen a prefiguring of the Trinity, three angelic visitors come to Abraham and Sarah. They are said to be an appearance of "the Lord," and they speak and act as one. In the icon they are pictured seated at the table provided by the hospitality of Sarah and Abraham. The figures appear lovingly inclined toward one another. They seem to be peacefully attentive to each other, distinct persons in a dynamic communion of love, engaged in a holy communion that is radically open. The holy conversation at that table creates a space for the viewer, for us. We are invited into a transforming relationship with God and one another. Ultimately we call this eternal life.

The unity of God (i.e., the Trinity) is neither static nor simple. Neither is our life in union with God. To speak of the One God in Three Persons is to speak of the fullness of God's life as a kind of dynamic tension between differentiation and unity. This is expressed by the self-giving of Father, Son, and Holy Spirit. In the icon of the Trinity, the cup on the table represents sacrifice. There is no healing, in other words, apart from encountering the boundaries of what it means to be a person, the self-giving required to be in relationship with other persons. Healing humankind as made in the image of God means embracing our diversity, the life-giving tensions that come with it, and the sacrifices required to sustain community. It means coming to regard diversity and tension in light of the love of God revealed to us in Christ Jesus. In a world of instant communication, fragmenting cultures, and massive weaponry, the stakes have never been higher. The very future of humanity may depend on cultivating a reverence for what Rabbi Jonathan Sacks calls the "Dignity of Difference."[5] The wellness of creation requires it.

The church is an outward and visible sign of the mystery of Christ. Sacramental signs serve to communicate the reality to which they point. Healthy and well-differentiated relationships within the church signify the dynamic love of God in Christ which makes itself vulnerable to the wounds of the world. Healthy relationships—with others and with the self—make for a resilient diversity that is capable of meeting, embracing, and transforming pain and confusion, no small matter in a world of rapid change and chronic anxiety. Again, the human body provides an analogy. As the writer David Whyte points out, a healthy heartbeat is constantly changing, responding to stimuli and interacting with other physical and emotional processes.[6] A sure sign of a heart about to die is an unresponsively dull, unwavering beat. Over time, a healthy heart, constantly subject to fluctuations and changes in rhythm, demonstrates a remarkably stable pattern. In a healthy body, organs and systems exist in complementary relationships capable of adapting and responding to challenges and change. Resiliency is a reliable indicator of good health and the diversity in which it is rooted.

Diversity, the source of what makes us strange to one another and even to ourselves, the disfiguring of which is the root of hatred and war, can also be healed into an image of Divinity. As the Jewish mystical tradition has it, "Unity in heaven creates diversity on earth."[7] Christ entered the full particularity of our human life, with its weaknesses and joys and sorrows. Jesus knew himself as a distinct individual in a particular time and place, in a world where hope for an abundant life was systematically crushed under the weight of oppressive political and religious systems. "Christ emptied himself," says the letter to the Philippians, "taking the form of a servant." (Philippians 2:8) In Christ, God took on our human nature, emptying himself into our wounded condition. He walked through a world where distinctions and diversity were kept under oppressive control. He touched those who were not supposed to be touched. He accepted and healed those who were supposed to be beyond hope. He died rather than make anyone else a victim. So the wholeness of humanity, its ultimate healing and reconciliation, does not require the elimination of differences or even conflict. It does require a transformed will and heart. It requires the "mind of Christ" who gave himself for others, who offered himself to God. Christ "emptied himself," not clinging even to his own divine selfhood.

Healing the Self

Twenty years ago my son was born two months early. Jonathan was a strong baby and we were lucky that he was born without many of the complications that many premature infants suffer. He was, however, born with a particular congenital abnormality: he was born without a left hand. In the weeks following his birth I had a recurring dream in which the central figure was a little boy with two hands. I quickly figured out the meaning of the dream (or so I thought) by concluding that the little boy in the dream was a flawless, fantasy version of my son. I decided that God was telling me I needed to let go of that "perfect" fantasy child in order to embrace the reality of my son. A friend of mine, who was as much a spiritual director to me as anyone, listened to the story of my son's birth and the recurring dream and the sense I had made of it all, and then rearranged my spiritual landscape. He understood what I thought the dream was telling me, but then he told me I was wrong. It wasn't a fantasy version of my son in the dream; it was a perfect fantasy version of myself. My son was and is just fine the way he is—it was me God wanted to heal. God was inviting me to release the impossible standards of perfection and performance I demand of myself. Ultimately, it was an invitation to heal me of the many ways I attempt to play at being God.

Accepting my own partiality, my own incompleteness, my creatureliness, the tension created by my weaknesses, is part of the work of salvation within me. It is an aspect of sustaining a healthy sense of self. Acceptance is not the same thing as the compulsive focus our culture puts on techniques for "self-improvement," rather it is a clear and honest view of myself in the light of Christ's love for me. In the twelfth century, St. Bernard of Clairvaux spoke of four degrees of love.

There is the first infantile stage of "love of self for the sake of self." "Give me that bottle!" We may progress to the next stage of "love of the other for the sake of self. "Oh, *you* gave me that bottle." And so on to the more or less selfless stage of "love of the other for the sake of the other." This is the place of genuine human love, a reflection of the love of God, the place of altruism. But, says Bernard, there is a final stage which is heaven's healing. This is the "love of self only for the sake of the Other." Knowing this love is to arrive at a true image of myself, a measure of the view God has of me, to see myself to some degree in the way the One who loves me into being sees me.[8]

Practicing Abundant Life

The church is called to be a communicating sign, a sacramental agent of the desire of Christ for this world. We pray our theology. We do it. We are called to practice what we pray so that our words will take on flesh and blood. Wellness, wholeness, abundant life is the will of God for all God's people. Abundant life should be observable in the baptized community. People should be able to taste it and touch it. The Baptismal Covenant of the Episcopal Church commits all the members of the church to practices that support and sustain the health of the Body of Christ, practices that aim to make God's healing love not simply true, but also real. "Will you do all in your power to uphold these persons in their life in Christ?" we ask. "Will you seek and serve Christ in all persons, loving your neighbor as yourself?" Respect for the integrity, the dignity of every human person is central to the baptismal promises. The Eucharistic assembly is a model of differentiated unity—all the members of the church take distinctive roles in the celebration, and all are needed so that the meal may be shared, the Body nourished and empowered for mission.

Churches have taken important steps to ensure that all their members can live in safety. Intentional ministries of health and wholeness have arisen in many places. For physicians, nurses, and other healthcare professionals, there is an increasing interest in the importance of spirituality and the life of prayer in achieving and sustaining health. Prayer groups and ministers of healing are rediscovering the riches of our tradition in the laying on of hands and anointing. There is a growing recognition that genuine health depends on the interdependence and integration of mind, body, and spirit, and that promoting this integration is the business of the whole church. Promoting the health, reconciliation, and well-being of the world requires a church of richly diverse gifts, praying constantly for its own reconciliation, healing, and conversion to Christ.

 oxo

Notes

1. Christmas Message from the Archbishop of Canterbury, December 17, 2008.

2. Olivier Clément, *The Roots of Christian Mysticism* (Hyde Park, NY: New City Press, 1993), 263.

3. Ibid., 265.

4. Willy Rordorf, et al., *The Eucharist of the Early Christians* (Liturgical Press, 1978), 61.

5. Jonathan Sacks, *The Dignity of Difference: How to Avoid the Clash of Civilization* (New York: Continuum, 2002).

6. David Whyte, *The Heart Aroused: Poetry and the Preservation of the Soul in Corporate America* (Random House, 2002), 226f.

7. Sacks, *The Dignity of Difference*, 54.

8. *On the Love of God*, online version at Christian Classics Ethereal Library.

Values To Live By

Robert R. Hansel

In the past twenty-five years or so, in various areas of American society, there has been a lot of talk about values. It has been alleged by some observers that there has been a national "decline in values," resulting in moral chaos, a decline in positive work performance standards, and even an increase in criminality. Some people want nationwide enforcement of the "right" values, those standards of thought and behavior to which all members of society should be held. Others vehemently reject that notion, viewing it as an infringement of personal rights and freedom. For them, values must remain personal beliefs and opinions.

Regardless of such differing views, values are generally understood to be a good thing. Most people would agree that a truly healthy, whole, well person (or community) is one that consistently holds to sound principles of living. Such standards are like a compass, helping people steer a life-course that is responsible and meaningful.

In the 1970s Dr. Sidney Simon of Temple University, along with Louis Rath, published the most popular and widely read study on the subject of values—a book titled *Values and Teaching*, followed by *Values Clarification* and *The Search for Values*. The authors sought to differentiate between mere "personal choices" such as selecting chocolate ice cream over vanilla and those deeply held priorities that underlie and govern our most critically important personal life-shaping decisions as well as providing a basis for communal life. Their basic insight was that there are distinct qualities that separate the two and that persons who are seeking "wellness"—individuals who want to be intentional, consistent, and effective in life—need to take the time to recognize, understand, and act on the basis of their own deeply held set of core values.

Everyone recognizes that core values are very tricky things. We may *think* that we're guided by a particular set of priorities when, in fact, it may be that we're actually being led by pressures or desires that are antithetical to what we claim. So how can a person know? The criteria that Simon and Rath offer have proved to be a relatively simple and effective way for an individual to discern those principles (or values) upon which to base personal decisions and, for that matter, decisions which operate corporately within societies, institutions, and organizations.

Let's consider one example. Suppose that I claim that I am committed to the principle that "all people are created equal." That statement suggests that I am always guided by that belief in determining my actions and decisions. To determine if this really *is* a value upon which my life is solidly based, here are seven criteria against which to test the depth of my views regarding human equality:

1. Was that view chosen freely without pressure, punishment, or threat?

2. Was that view selected from among other known alternatives?

3. Was that view chosen with full awareness of possible consequences?

4. Do I cherish and prize the choice that I have made in this regard?

5. Am I ready to affirm my view aloud in public?

6. Will I act on my choice when it costs something to do so?

7. Have I, over a long period of time, consistently held and acted on this view?

Clearly these are tough, demanding standards of the "stand up and be counted" sort. That's precisely their purpose—to separate the most important and highest principles from the arbitrary and inconsequential. Personal and societal values are developed only through a lifetime of experience and reflection, as we consider truthfully, carefully, and prayerfully what we actually *are*, not just what we would like to be or what we wish that we were.

The only way to avoid a life of confusion, being torn between arbitrary priorities and making decisions that are completely random, is to find a set of values that is both positive and dependable. A person who is living in a state of wellness—a life characterized by strong, healthy, consistent standards of what truly matters—is someone who has taken the time to understand and affirm his/her authentic priorities. Rather than, as The Book of Common Prayer states so graphically in a Sunday Collect, "being blown about by every changing wind of doctrine," the person who is truly well is guided by commitments that, when pursued consistently, have been demonstrated to bring a sense of purpose, fulfillment, and satisfaction.

So, what are the core values that lie at the heart of the Christian faith? What are the core values of our faith that promote authentic wellness? Certainly to the general criteria to determine core values offered above, the Christian standard would insist on an additional item that asks, "Is this consistent with what we know of the model given to us in the life of Jesus Christ?" Beginning with that one addition to the criteria for identifying a core value, I want to suggest that there is, indeed, a set of implicit Christian core values. While individual Christians certainly might, understandably, differ on those specifics, I want to offer here what seem to me to be the basic core values that, throughout the centuries, the Christian faith has found to profoundly underlie and sustain human wellness:

1. *Commitment to living as a Christ-centered person and seeking to build intentionally Christ-centered communities.*

   This is the primary Christian commitment, upon which everything else depends; therefore it is critical that there should be absolute clarity about its meaning. Perhaps the best way to define the term, *Christ-centered*, would be to point out that genuine Christian faith is based on a personal relationship, rather than upon some set of narrowly defined religious doctrines requiring our intellectual assent. Christian faith proceeds from an experience of relationship—a sense of our being "people in a Presence." The resurrection of Jesus means that Christ is alive and active right now in the heart and mind of every person on this planet. Being a Christian means being in touch with that presence every day—knowing and seeking to be constantly faithful to our "life in Christ."

   Clearly, God's unique action initiates and precedes any human response. Each individual Christian comes out of a lifelong journey of faith that has led him/her to know Christ in a profound way, unique to himself/herself. Yet, there are some basic common experiences that shape the way in which all Christians have come to know God in and through Christ. Whatever else Jesus Christ showed to us in his life and ministry, there are his primary commitments of faithfulness, gratitude, and love. In Jesus we see absolute trust in the will and purposes of God, a pervasive, thankful stewardship of every gift of this life, and a total unselfishness manifested in compassion and practical action on behalf of anyone who is in need or at risk.

A Christian, pure and simple, is one who sees in that unique model of THANKSliving exactly what it means to be effective in his/her witness to God's initiative. Although living up to that high standard is impossible for us to attain relying only on our own resources, Christians are convinced that Christ both empowers and forgives. God gives us strength to transcend our limitations and we are forgiven when our best efforts fall short of the mark. Christians rely on the absolute certainty of Jesus Christ's continuing presence whenever we, in caring community, work together to "seek and serve Christ in all persons."

Following the example of Jesus, the Christian church—at its best—challenges all people to build and strengthen their own personal faith in the ways that are most helpful and meaningful for themselves, never insisting on some narrowly theological interpretation. The strategy is to "respect the dignity of every human being" by affirming each person's own calling as a sacred trust to be nurtured and revered. Such openness to a range of understanding and interpretation is a scary prospect for some. They want to restrict such freedom by insisting on creedal uniformity. The result is the emergence, today, in every era of Church history, a precarious tension between individual and institutional needs. The institution constantly threatens to impose the dead hand of outdated dogma upon the life-giving freshness of God's ongoing revelation. It all seems to work best when the institution has a high tolerance for variety, insisting on only the most non-negotiable tenets of belief. The church, in this view, always seeks to create an atmosphere in which conditions are maximized for Christ's healing presence to flow. The assumption is that each participant is committed to the highest standard of personal stewardship—to seek a state of personal and professional wellness in which nothing hinders the most effective response to God's calling. The goal is to offer assistance and empowerment, reaching out to another without concern for personal gain.

Institutional titles, rank, and status have very little importance in the Christ-centered life. Church politics get left behind. Any notion of self-appointed "experts" telling others what to think or do has limited application. At best these are resources, springboards for personal reflection and growth. Leading and learning are roles handed back and forth because we understand that "the Spirit flows where it will" and Christ's presence will redeem and transform all of us into a community of shared service. That norm, in short, represents a primary core value that we find reflected in the church when it is truly well transforming and enriching our individual and institutional ministry throughout the entire world.

2. *Commitment to the pursuit of unifying the heart, mind, body, and spirit.*

There are many programs of personal and vocational "training" available for the continuing growth and education of the church's ordained and lay leaders and members. Most of those programs address some particular area of function or skill—new strategies for raising money, physical exercise activities for better health, or for more effective preaching tips for next Lent. While there certainly is a need for such education, this second core value of Christian faith holds that genuine wellness can only be found in an integration of every facet of the whole person, not just the intellect or the talents in isolation, but every aspect of one's being working together in a unity of focus. Unity with God and with one another begins with a sense of personal integrity.

For years church wellness initiatives have unmistakably revealed that one's own wellness is most threatened by any imbalance that favors work over leisure, job over family, intellect over exercise. Christian faith values equally all facets of human life and experience. Physical wellness and activity are not "inferior" to intellectual or aesthetic qualities. It is in the balance, unity, and harmony of the entire person (or community) that true wellness emerges. For Christians, the ultimate goal of life is, through Christ, to be restored to complete unity with God—a harmony in which all the fragmentation and division that cause self-alienation and separates people from one another is finally overcome. The authentic Christian community seeks to involve participants in a total renewal experience, one in which their faith, their work, their relationships, and their physical well-being find integration and refreshment. The very same root linguistic source word is shared by "wholeness," "holiness," "happiness," and "health." Christians are committed to the core value of challenging and breaking down the compartmentalization that often separates work from bliss, home and family from job, desires from duties, and the realm of the spiritual from ordinary reality. Instead, the church offers an opportunity and a variety of resources by which members can journey toward a more complete drawing-together of every gift that God has given them. For

Christians, one of the most strongly held values is a belief that God created us to find our true selves in a unity that defies fragmentation. Conversely, alienation, loneliness, and isolation result from a failure to see the interconnectedness of one's entire being. Lasting wellness and personal peace come only from the integration of all aspects of one's life. In the end, of course, such renewal is the work of God alone. Our privilege is to offer resources, support, and assistance and then to get out of the Spirit's way.

3. *Commitment to an understanding that we are all part of a living stream with a sustainable spirit.*

The revelation of the nature and purpose of God that flowed from the life and ministry of Jesus is not yet complete. God continues to open new visions and insights every day. A third Christian core value is the perception that our experience of God is still growing, changing, and being discovered. Like our experience of a parent, a friend, a child, or a spouse undergoes daily enrichment and deepening, so is our apprehension and appreciation of God. While we can trace patterns that provide assurance and trust, the process of discovery is not yet complete.

No one should presume to think that he has arrived at some eternal, immutable truth that we need to protect, preserve, and transmit to others. Rather, a Christian core value is to see ourselves as always engaged in a continuing quest that responds to God's constantly changing and challenging call. The church invites people to immerse themselves into that flowing stream. It is that spirit of adventure and discovery that enlivens healthy Christian community at every level of its programmatic and institutional life. Although there is certainly a legitimate level of history and tested structure within the life of the church, its liveliness and spontaneity depend on leaders, and participants' willingness to throw all our plans up in the air and reassemble them in light of God's new gifts of insight and creativity. That very process is the evidence that God's spirit is present within us and our community, creating, sustaining, and extending our work. For that reason, controversy and conflict are normal elements of wellness of Christian community.

God brings out of our differences and disagreements the new thing that is promised throughout Holy Scriptures. Far from seeking some homogenized and apathetic uniformity, the wellness that is valued is a restlessly creative energy requiring patience, understanding, and tolerance. As it pursues personal and corporate wellness, our experience of Christian faith will be a vital part of a learning experience that continues to be shared and by which all are sustained in their practice of ministry.

4. *Commitment to a disciplined reflective lifecycle process of identity, discernment, practice, and transformation.*

Central to every Christian pursuit of wellness is the practice of a reflective process, the four steps of which can be identified as IDPT·

*I*dentity: Who and what am I right at this minute in time—with all my faults and all my gifts? How do I understand myself, my relationships, and my responsibilities?

*D*iscernment: Who and what is God calling me to be?

*P*ractice: How am I responding to God's call? What am I doing to be more faithful and effective? What resources are there to help me?

*T*ransformation: How am I changing and being changed by God's spirit within me as I seek to follow a new practice and pattern of faithful ministry?

Some individuals have a seemingly innate, unconscious gift by which this practice of wellness renewal appears simply to have "always been there." For others, it is a learned, conscious discipline. Whichever the case, a core value of Christian wellness holds that the daily application of IDPT for personal and professional growth is central to a lifelong process of personal and vocational renewal. Just as importantly, it is a discipline that the entire Christian church is called to apply to its total corporate life.

Every institution—a business, a religious congregation, a government, or an entire society—is constantly at risk of becoming fossilized. Without constant reassessment and renewal, practices and policies become set in concrete and can actually prevent progress if we're not mindful. Wellness—personal or corporate—demands change and we must embrace the challenge of new ways of thinking about old truths if we are to remain vital. No doubt, this is a demanding and even risky perspective—one that is often rejected by the defenders of an unchanging, eternal view of the Word of God. While ultimate truth does not change, its expression and relevance always have to be rearticulated and made applicable to changed circumstances. The alternative is a nit-picking devotion to perpetuating the minutiae of religious lore. Such fearful resistance to anything new cannot be consistent with our experience of the renewing energy of God. The entire Christian revelation—the new covenant—proceeds from the very notion that time after time peoples and religions have lost their vitality and turned into museums. It is God's will throughout history to break through like "new wine in old wineskins" to refresh and renew.

Christian faith places a very high value on the IDPT model of reflection, learning, and change. All Christians are called, in their own way, to take the time to "do their IDPT." It's the only way we can be sure that we stay open to God's spirit. It's the only way we can continue to keep up with the God who moves ahead of us every day, boldly doing a new thing.

It's Who We Are.

It is my firm belief that by seeking to be true to these four core values, the Christian faith points the way toward authentic human wellness. Over two thousand years of experiences, these four core values have been shown to build sound practical principles of teaching, learning, affirming, showing hospitality, worshiping, and serving for which we think God has raised us up. History shows us innumerable authentic Christians and authentic church communities that achieve greatness by seeking to pursue these same beliefs and commitments. That's why I confidently identify these four essential commitments as our Christian "core values."

Toward a Theology of Identity

Michael J. Battle

Who is God calling you to be? Isaiah answers through the imagery of mighty waters suddenly appearing in the desert. It is as if for Isaiah God is calling us forth to discover a new identity through impossible circumstances. Even in a desert, nothing can prevent the mighty waters from springing forth, producing something new, even a garden in a wasteland. (Isaiah 43:19) In this chapter, I invite you to step with me into the waters of identity. In these often-troubled waters we immediately discover a theological paradox—namely, a person cannot discover self-identity alone. This is a paradox because self-identity implies solitude and isolation; so how can anyone discover self through any other means than through self? As we aim our toes toward these murky waters of identity, let us prepare for surprises—by doing so, we will increase our wellness. In short, I think we learn from God's own identity that identity cannot be discovered in the vacuum of self; rather, self-identity will always need the healthy reference points of others in community.

Misnomer of "Self-Identity"

Self-identity is not a possession about which one can say: There it is. God has made us in the divine image that is not static and yet is identifiable. I like to put it this way: Self is a responsible mystery! Instead of relegating self to the mysterious because we lack the will to analyze such existence deeply, I argue that self is a responsible mystery in which we are called to go as deep as we can, knowing that we can never reach the bottom. In this way, self-identity is always in pursuit of new life—that is to say, a new world of possibilities, one that is to be constructed day by day. Identity, after all, implies movement and growth. And perhaps this rather obvious point is an indicator of what must be central for any adequate understanding of wellness. Self-identity is a misnomer in the sense that no one can introspectively know self. There needs to be a reference point, as the following story illustrates.

33

One Sunday morning, everyone in one bright, beautiful, tiny town got up early and went to church. Before the services started, the townspeople were sitting in their pews and talking about the mundane details of their lives. Suddenly, Satan appeared at the front of the church. Everyone started screaming and running for the exits, trampling each other in a frantic effort to get away from evil incarnate.

Soon the church was empty, except for one elderly lady who sat calmly in her pew, not moving . . . seemingly oblivious to the fact that God's ultimate enemy was in her presence. Now, this confused Satan a bit, so he walked up to the woman and said, "Don't you know who I am?"

The woman replied, "Yep, sure do."

Satan asked, "Aren't you afraid of me?"

"Nope, sure ain't," said the woman.

Satan was a little perturbed at this and queried, "Why aren't you afraid of me?"

The woman calmly replied, "Been married to your brother for over forty-eight years."

Even Jesus asked, "Who do they say I am?" (Matthew 16:13) The discovery of self is a relational journey. Jesus, Paul, and other writers in scripture stressed the themes of the call to mature identity in community and the risks of regression into self-absorption. For example, the opening chapters of I Corinthians remind a community of self-satisfied and fractious converts that they are chosen in the first place for their weakness (I. 26:31) and that their calling is to an ever greater identification with the humility and hiddenness of God's action in Christ (I. 17–25, 2: 1–9). This (2:6) is their maturity and their wisdom—a maturity which their various self-assertions amply show they do not possess (3:1–4). Ultimately, in Christian theology, Christ reveals the way to discover identity through community. Such a way is not always easy, however.

Murky Waters of Identity

Because it is frightening and painful to be confronted with the awareness that our belief in a controlled sense of self may often be empty and self-serving, we readily turn away and often embrace unauthentic lives. To save us from such hell, God often provokes a crisis to destroy our self-deceiving reliance. In other words, we cannot figure out life by ourselves and soon discover we need help. So, if we think we see ourselves clearly, God often muddies our waters so that we do not settle on superficial self-identity. Paul himself had to struggle through the murky process of finding his identity, as his eyes were open and yet he could not see. (Acts 9:8) In fact, Paul needed someone else (Ananias) to become aware of his new identity. (Acts 9:17) Paul took his new name and identity through the grace of Christian community:

> For by the grace given to me I say to everyone among you not to think of yourself more highly than you ought to think, but to think with sober judgment, each according to the measure of faith that God has assigned. For as in one body we have many members, and not all the members have the same function, so we, who are many, are one body in Christ, and individually we are members one of another. (Romans 12: 3–5)

People formed through Christ's discipleship believe, deep in the core of their being, that God loved humanity into being. God's love is prevenient—it is there before everything else and calls all of our justifications for control of identity into account. In short, as a Christian, no one can claim full control of her or his life. "We see through a mirror dimly." (1 Corinthians 13:12) The Christian accepts the need to be transformed into a new identity, a new perspective articulated by Archbishop Desmond Tutu:

> God does not love us because we are lovable, but we are lovable precisely because God loves us. God's love is what gives us our worth. . . . So we are liberated from the desire to achieve, to impress. We are the children of the divine love and nothing can change that fundamental fact about us.[1]

It is in this understanding of God's love and human identity that we can then make sense of one of the most fascinating concepts of the twenty-first century, Ubuntu. Archbishop Tutu's Ubuntu theology allows access to a new identity for South Africans, especially as he appeals to ancient African concepts of individual and community which John Mbiti sums up in the following statement: "I am because we are, and since we are, therefore I am."[2]

Ubuntu

Real unity of the individual depends on the unity of the community. I think this is why the 2008 Lambeth Conference was designed around Indaba Groups, which are small groups designed around the African concept of forming consensus through communal conversation, rather than the deductive processes that often accompany gatherings in the Western world. African spirituality begins with community and moves to individuality, whereas Western spirituality tends to move from individuality to community. Western definitions of "community" usually mean something like a collection of self-interested people, each with a private set of preferences, all of whom get together because they realize that in association they can accomplish things that they are not able to accomplish otherwise. This definition of community is actually an aggregation, a sum of individuals. Not only does this go against the African view of community but, methodologically, this Western definition of community becomes a tautology or a circular argument. In other words, Western definitions of community are based primarily on individuality. Individuals pick and choose their own definitions of community. This, however, is not the African concept of community. John Mbiti's aphorism: "I am because we are" suggests a thoroughly fused collective "we." This lesson of African community is strange for us in competitive Western cultures. Caught in the competitive schemes of the Western world, i.e., between materialism and spirituality, and between individualism and collectivism, the contribution of Ubuntu is in its display of a symbiosis between individual and community. Tutu explains this symbiosis through an African idiom—a person is a person through other persons. We are made for interdependence. Archbishop Tutu eloquently describes this symbiosis:

> We find that we are placed in a delicate network of vital relationship with the Divine, with my fellow human beings and with the rest of creation. . . . We are meant then to live as members of one family, the human family exhibiting a rich diversity of attributes and gifts in our differing cultures as members of different races and coming from different milieus—and precisely because of this diversity, made for interdependence.

> [T]he peace we want is something positive and dynamic. In the Hebrew it is called *shalom*, which refers to wholeness, integrity; it

means well being, physical and spiritual. It means the abundance of life which Jesus Christ promised He had brought. It has all to do with a harmonious coexistence with one's neighbors in a wholesome environment allowing persons to become more fully human.[3]

The totally self-sufficient human being does not exist. We all need others in order to be human. That is why the cutthroat competitiveness of the so-called free enterprise system is so disturbing for Africans such as Tutu [4] People should not compete against one another to know who they are; rather, we should cooperate in order to know who we are. Tutu explains this problem through an example of how Western culture tends to depend on competition to form human identity:

> [O]ne day at a party in England for some reason we were expected to pay for our tea. I offered to buy a cup for an acquaintance. Now, he could have said: "No, thank you." You could have knocked me down with a feather when he replied, "No, I won't be subsidized!" Well, I never. I suppose it was an understandable attitude. You want to pay your own way and not sponge on others. But it is an attitude that many have seemed to carry over into our relationship with God— our refusal to be subsidized by God. It all stems very much from the prevailing achievement ethic which permeates our very existence. It is drummed into our heads from our most impressionable days that you must succeed. At school you must not just do well, no you must grind the opposition into the dust. We get so worked up that our children can become nervous wrecks as they are egged on to greater efforts by competitive parents. Our culture has it that ulcers have become status symbols.[5]

There is something seriously wrong with a system which encourages a high degree of competitiveness and selfishness in a world where we seem to have been made for interdependence. Something is clearly wrong about a system of people whose goal is to achieve success despite the result of dehumanization. More provocatively, competition is the sign of the fall of creation and it is the opposite of Ubuntu. Tutu concludes:

> Have you seen a symphony orchestra? They are all dolled up and beautiful with their magnificent instruments, cellos, violins, etc. Sometimes dolled up as the rest, is a chap at the back carrying a triangle. Now and again the conductor will point to him and he will

play "ting." That might seem so insignificant but in the conception of the composer something irreplaceable would be lost to the total beauty of the symphony if that "ting" did not happen.[6]

Ultimately, Ubuntu concerns the integrity of being human before God. We learn to be human from the most humane person, Jesus Christ. In Christ we discover someone who is fully human and fully God. To know this perfect humanity of Christ, however, requires the paradox of knowing self-identity in which our knowledge is dependent on a community (the church) who, being diverse and yet one, seeks to live in the mystery of the image of God. Ubuntu is the quality of interaction in which one's own humanness depends upon recognition of the humanness of the other. In the end, Ubuntu gives us the insight that human endeavor is meant to be shared. We forget this at our peril. The beauty of Archbishop Tutu's understanding of Ubuntu is that it offers an alternative model to our Western individualism. Ubuntu gives us encouragement that, as Christians, we are bidden by the imperatives of our biblical faith to realize our connectedness as God's children. The appeal for Ubuntu for us is not for an appeal against individual uniqueness, but more specifically to the mystery of persons (i.e., in God and creation). Ubuntu theology is formed around the fact that there is so much about another person which cannot be known and cannot be known without community. Tutu turns the concept of Ubuntu into a theological concept in which human beings are called to be persons because we are made in the image of God. Tutu concludes, "[Regarding the recording of a symphony] If it was only one person it would be alright. But it is glorious when it is a harmony, a harmony of different voices. Glorious. God is smart. God says it is precisely our diversity that makes for our unity. It is precisely because you are you and I am me that [God] says, 'you hold on together.'"[7]

Conclusion and Challenge

We discover self-identity as we discover community. Such community should make us more authentically ourselves. As I speak around the country, often on the topic of reconciliation and the spirituality of community, I am inevitably challenged about my argument that self-identity is discovered in community. The challenge carries force as someone in the audience wants to know about communities that may not necessarily be healthy for individuals. Patricia Cranton illustrates this assumption through the problem of being an authentic teacher in the classroom:

I recently discussed the idea of being an authentic teacher with a seasoned science education professor—a man who was looking forward to retirement within the next year after thirty years of teaching practice. He was almost appalled at the notion of being oneself with students. "I don't think I could go for that," he said, startled by what he saw as my naiveté. "Who I am in the classroom and who I am outside of the classroom are two different people. Students don't need to know me, they need to know how to teach science." Perhaps my raising the topic provoked images of personal self-disclosure or an emotional sharing of feelings with students, things that had no place in his mind in science teaching, but more likely, he simply saw teaching as something he does rather than who he is.[8]

In her book, *Becoming an Authentic Teacher in Higher Education*, Patricia Cranton is ambivalent about self-identity for all the reasons mentioned so far concerning Western cultures. Cranton is especially instructive to the enterprise of how one discovers identity. Such identity is not primarily discovered through the dispensing of information but through formation and transformation.

I have argued that self-identity must be discovered in relationship. In order to be a healthy person, you need a community; you cannot know you are handsome or beautiful, intelligent or wise, without the reference point of someone else to provide you such perspective. Other persons can help us truly see ourselves. We are not to live life as if we are playing a role. Most importantly, playing a role cannot maintain authentic interaction needed in the demanding tasks of ministry. When we grow toward a clearer perception of ourselves as individuals in healthy community, we inevitably invite others to do the same.

This is why we pray together. By prayer I understand something like maturing in the reality of God. Such prayer is not something easily said, but something that must be done. But we typically understand prayer the other way around, as something that is seldom done and more often only said. This is why there are so many books on prayer and so little demonstration of it. So, movement toward a theology of identity is about preparing a person to mature in the life of God—the ultimate community. The mystics and spiritual writers help us see that we are preparing for an experience we cannot evoke when we look for self-identity. "Contemplation," says Richard of St. Victor, "is a free and clear vision of the mind fixed upon the manifestation of wisdom in suspended wonder." Such contemplation, however, does not end with self. Because of the reference point of God both in us and beyond us, our vision of self-identity is made whole. This is a paradox—a gift from God.

☙❧

Notes

1. Archbishop Desmond Tutu, Handwritten Sermons, at St. Phillip's, Washington D.C., Christmas III, 1984.

2. John Mbiti, *African Religions and Philosophies* (New York: Doubleday and Company, 1970), 141.

3. Tutu, Address, "The Quest for Peace," Johannesburg, August 1986.

4. Tutu, "Postcript: To Be Human is To Be Free," 317.

5. Tutu, Addresses and Speeches, "What Jesus Means to Me," Durban University, August 6–7, 1981.

6. Tutu, "What Jesus Means to Me."

7. Transcript of Tutu's Sermon in Birmingham Cathedral, April 21, 1988. Published by: Committee for Black Affairs, Birmingham, Diocesan Office, 4–5.

8. Patricia Cranton, *Becoming an Authentic Teacher in Higher Education* (Malabar, FL: Krieger Publishing Company, 2001), 43.

The Relationships of Identity to Wellness

"Know Thyself," Be Yourself, Connect Yourself

Mathew L. Sheep

When I discover who I am, I'll be free.

—Ralph Ellison[1]

Even in contemporary times, the ancient Greek admonition to "know thyself" can be a wellspring of strength and wellness for those who have taken the pains to do so and an exigency for those who have not. In its best sense, "know thyself" is a call to effectiveness, to enhancing the lives of others—through service, leadership, and counsel. Of course, there are critics of the quest for self-awareness. Andre Gide wrote: "Whoever studies himself arrests his own development. A caterpillar who seeks to know himself would never become a butterfly." Such wisdom is a good stance only if one is addicted to the superficial logic of the online quotation databases (which is where I found this one—www.brainyquote.com—I'm not addicted). However, we might also argue that, for the caterpillar to "know herself" well, she must also know that she possesses the potential to transform into her future self—the butterfly. The caterpillar does not know her identity adequately for current circumstances unless she also knows something of the future state she is in the process of becoming—and, barring any unforeseen cocoon mishaps—will become. Thus, knowing oneself both actually and potentially (and not getting the two confused) can lead to more positive experiences regarding outcomes in the world.

Similarly, it is also important for groups and organizations to know who they are. A clear and commonly shared concept of identity is often at the heart of both individual and collective wellness. In my experience as an ordained minister, I served in three congregations over a twenty-year period. During that time, I came to understand that not all congregations have clear perceptions of their organizational identities—their central, distinctive, and relatively enduring characteristics.[2] Whether the organization's identity is experienced as monolithic or inclusive was

41

not really the issue. Instead, congregations were helped or hindered in mission largely as a result of the shared clarity of their identity—who are we? What are we all about? For whom are we here?

The questions are simple, the answers are complex. I will never forget a remark made to me by an architectural planning consultant immediately following a meeting in which he had presented to our building committee plans for an addition to our existing facility. In a very perplexed tone of voice, he whispered to me, "There were a lot of different paradigms in that room tonight."

His observation represented for me the identity challenges that many, if not most, congregations face today as they seek to navigate the rapid cultural and environmental currents that shape ministry. During that meeting, even though the consultant had clearly articulated the nature and purpose of the new facility, it became apparent that little consensus existed among the committee members. One member advocated the add-on as a gym for teenagers and young adults; another feared it would become a venue for rock concerts; another saw it as a new worship space; and yet another as a "family life" activity center. Rather than seeing these uses as complementary, committee members regarded them as conflicting or threatening to their perceptions of the congregation's identity. What was interesting is that these diverse building uses symbolized competing perceptions of *how* the congregation's identity was changing, and the reasons *why* it should or should not change.

Some congregations face the predicament of having at one time shared a collective understanding of identity, but their environment has changed dramatically, leaving members unsure of how the traditionally defined identity will adjust to new cultural realities. Consequently, they may develop divergent understandings of the congregation's identity. Identity *divergence* (not the same as diversity) has an impact on the organization's effectiveness.

The key assumption undergirding the discussion of identity in this chapter is this: Healthy individuals and organizations can navigate change, weather storms, and serve others more effectively than those that are less healthy. Moreover, health and overall wellness can often lead to a harmonious answer to the question, "Who do we say that we are?" It is no coincidence that the question resembles the identity-question of Jesus to Peter: "Who do people say that the Son of Man is?" (Matthew 16:13)

Regardless of its theological implications, the very asking of the question is remarkable in that it acknowledges identity as not simply an internal state but a communicated message. It is both sent and received—a phenomenon that is constructed (whether as intended or not) in and through interaction with others. "Who I am" as well as "who we are" must be received, attended to, and acted upon *by others* for identity to be enacted in the world as a social reality.

It should come as little surprise, then, that identity is a complex topic. First, it can have multiple aspects within a single entity. Second, identity can be studied on a number of levels—individual, social, and organizational. Third, identity can change to adapt to changing circumstances in the environment to achieve certain outcomes—enhancement, growth, or even survival. In this chapter, we will examine the relationship of identity to wellness along these three dimensions: multiplicity, different levels, and change.

Multiple Aspects of Identity and Wellness: How Do I Manage the Many Me's?

Even though multiple aspects of identity may conflict, we nevertheless embody multiple aspects that can differ in saliency with the time and context. We may be "parent" in one context, "Little League coach" in another, and "chief financial officer" in yet another. These identities are based in different roles that we have, hats we wear.

With this in mind, my colleagues Glen Kreiner, Elaine Hollensbe, and I introduced a boundary approach to both individual and organizational identities that looks at identity at the edges—the interfaces between multiple aspects of identity both *within* a person or organization, as well as the interfaces *between* personal identities and the identities of an organization.[3] The effective integration or segmentation of multiple aspects of identity then becomes an issue of understanding and effectively managing the boundaries between them.

From this view, then, certain aspects of identity can have thick or permeable boundaries—where they mingle freely with other aspects or are very distinct and separate from them. Boundaries can be held in balance, or they may reflect imbalances with other identity aspects—for example, when an organization's identity demands too much of an individual's identity. ("I missed my son's graduation because my organization also defines itself as a family.") When an individual experiences a healthy overlap between his or her own identities and those of the organization, we refer to this as work-self balance. When a boundary loses balance, it can result in too much overlap (work-self intrusion) or not enough overlap (work-self distance). In work-self intrusion, the individual sees the organization's identity as invasive. In "work-self distance," there is not enough overlap—the individual longs for more oneness or identification with the organization's identity.[4]

The upshot of the boundary approach to wellness is that multiple aspects of both individual and organizational identity are interacting constantly in this way, sometimes placing great demands on the individual for identity boundary management. Such demands can affect psychological well-being and levels of stress and burnout.

Because research has generally supported the idea that both individuals and organizations may have multiple identities,[5] the prescription, especially in Western psychological research, is usually that multiple identities should be integrated into a coherent, consistent whole in order to be a "healthy" or well individual/organization. However, that notion is challenged somewhat in Eastern cultures, where "multiple selves" can be seen as co-existing realities held in a dialectical tension—with fewer negative effects on psychological well-being than in Western cultures.[6] More generally, identity multiplicity can provide for adaptability and effectiveness in a number of environments—thereby increasing subjective well-being in diverse contexts.

Identity and Wellness at Different Levels: The Butterfly Effect

Individual Identity and Wellness: "Know Thyself," Be Yourself

Individual identity relates to psychological concepts of self-knowledge or self-concept.

Although a matter of debate among psychologists, recent research has suggested that having a positive self-concept results in better performance as well as decreases in pathological outcomes such as depression and anxiety disorders.[7] Thus, a positive self-concept and identity are clearly linked to wellness outcomes.

A person who, for whatever reason, does *not* know himself or herself very well may know the *basics* of identity like name, gender, occupation, and associations with larger groups. However, such an individual is not aware of the aspects of identity that help or hinder participation in the world—aspects such as personal strengths, core values, and limitations—and the narratives of which one is a part. For example, an attempt to lead others without having some degree of self-knowledge can be a doomed enterprise. Expedition members who climb Everest, troops in perilous combat, employees of innovative technology firms, members in any kind of organization navigating the whitewater of change, are all dependent on leaders who have a clear knowledge of self-identity and what that identity will withstand under pressure.

If acting effectively in the world depends upon an honest examination/ assessment of self, then identity is a *crucial*, if not foundational component of wellness. "Who am I? What are my strengths and the approximate limits/ boundaries of my capacities and competencies? What am I becoming?" How we approach and then reflect upon answers to such questions influences one's own perceptions of well-being and mental/emotional wellness. In other words, if I have a clear sense of who I am, I can be more effective in my interactions in the world and in the accomplishment of my goals. That is not to say that I cannot stretch and grow, but it is to acknowledge where unacceptable risks lie and where successful accomplishments may occur. As a likely result, I will derive more *satisfaction* from my relatedness with "other(s)" and have a more healthy conception of self (e.g., in terms of self-efficacy, self-esteem, and reduced relational/ occupational stress).

Identity, Relationships, and Wellness: Connect Yourself to Others

Our construction of personal identity is not confined to a theatre of the mind that plays and replays self-concept formulations. To a far greater extent, "who we are" is shaped by our relationships with other people, groups, and organizations.

For example, individual identities may include "junior at Midvale High School," "honor roll student," "fan of hip-hop," "best friend of Michelle," "editor of school newspaper," and "Episcopalian." Some of these identities are based on collective identities (honor roll student) and some are based on common bonds (best friend of Michelle, Episcopalian). Some of our identifications are role-based (editor of school newspaper), while others are person-based (fan of hip-hop). *All* of them can impact in various ways our perceptions of self-esteem, self-concept, and even self-efficacy.[8] The standards that guide our conduct as well as our emotional well-being are derived from who we think we are in relation to others.[9]

Organizational Identity: Identifying Yourself with the Organization

> From this vantage point, collective visions of self, such as group and organizational identities, become not so much the "main show" as important resources in the formation of personal notions of self.[10]

As is increasingly recognized in the scholarly literature of identity studies, the individual level of identity is often analogous at the organizational level of identity.[11] That is to say, organizations not only have identities, but those identities are also constructed on a collective level in ways that resemble individual identity construction (e.g., identity construction is a negotiation at both levels). As with individuals, organizations that collectively share a clear understanding of the key components of their identity can interact more effectively in their specific contexts to engage in mission. In short, clearly shared conceptions of identity can foster both individual and organizational vitality.

The wellness of both organizations and individuals is also nurtured by the degree of members' identification with the organization. Identification with an organization occurs when members "define themselves at least partly in terms of what the organization is thought to represent."[12]

Identification is a perception of oneness with the organization that helps to define the self-concept. Thus, organizations are benefitted with loyal and committed members, and individual self-esteem and satisfaction is enhanced by association with an organization regarded to have a desirable identity.

Identity Transitions and Wellness:
Forgetting the Anguish, Enjoying the New

Lastly, we learned early in our biological education that all living things grow and change. We should expect the same thing in terms of an identity that reflects life and growth. Although identity has traditionally been thought to be more or less enduring and stable in both individuals and organizations, more recent research has challenged that notion.[13] Indeed, both individuals and organizations can and do change their identities for a variety of reasons.[14] Individuals, jobs, family circumstances, education levels, likes and dislikes all change—and their associated identities along with them. For organizations, competitive environments, strategies, products and services, ownership through mergers and acquisitions, all change—and their associated identities along with them. For congregations, dioceses, and even entire denominations, changes can occur that shape identity shifts at any or all levels—e.g., external cultural contexts, surrounding communities and demographic shifts, internal leadership initiatives and priorities, and historic events that both shape and are shaped by who we perceive ourselves to be.

How smoothly and effectively identity changes are navigated is an indicator of individual and organizational health—in the long run. Short-term conflicts and setbacks are nearly always a part of change because people, young and old alike, have many reasons for resisting change. We all like our comfort zones and a certain amount of stability—a deep structure that does not change.[15] Even so, as Jesus taught, even the joy that results from a change as significant as the birth of a new life involves pain, "but when her baby is born she forgets the anguish because of her joy that a child is born into the world." (John 16:21, NIV) One indication that an identity change is working toward individual and organizational wellness is that it may first involve some pain or discomfort, but it is followed by joy.

ෙᎧ

Notes

1. Ralph Ellison, *Invisible Man* (New York: Random House, Inc. 1995), 243.

2. S. Albert and D.A. Whetten. 1985. Organizational identity. In B. Staw & L. Cummings (Eds.), *Research in Organizational Behavior* 7: 263–295. Greenwich, CT: JAI Press.

3. G.E. Kreiner, E.C. Hollensbe, and M. Sheep. 2006. On the edge of identity: Boundary dynamics at the interface of individual and organization identities. *Human Relations*, 59(10): 1315–1341.

4. Ibid.

5. B.E. Ashforth and S.A. Johnson. Which hat to wear? The relative salience of multiple identities in organizational contexts. In M. A. Hogg & D. J. Terry (Eds.), *Social identity processes in organizational contexts* (Ann Arbor, MI: Taylor & Francis, 2001), 31–48; M.G. Pratt, and P.O. Foreman. Classifying managerial responses to multiple organizational identities. *Academy of Management Review*; 25, 18–42.

6. E.M. Suh. 2002. Culture, identity consistency, and subjective well-being. *Journal of Personality and Social Psychology* 83(6): 1378–1391.

7. W.B. Swan, Jr., C. Chang-Schneider, and K.L. McClarty. 2007. Do people's self-views matter? Self-concept and self-esteem in everyday life. *American Psychologist* 62(2): 84–94.

8. Who is this "we"? Levels of collective identity and self-representations. *Journal of Personality and Social Psychology*, 71–83–93.

9. E.T. Higgins. 1996. The "Self Digest": Self-knowledge serving self-regulatory functions. *Journal of Personality and Social Psychology* 71(6): 1062–1083.

10. M. Alvesson, K. Ashcraft, and R. Thomas. 2008. Identity matters: Reflections on the construction of identity scholarship in organization studies. *Organization* 15(1): 5–28.

11. D.A. Whetten. 2006. Albert and Whetten revisited: Strengthening the concept of organizational identity. *Journal of Management Inquiry* 15, 219–234.

12. G.E. Kreiner and B.E. Ashforth. 2004. Evidence toward an expanded model of organizational identification. *Journal of Organizational Behavior* 25: 1–27.

13. H.R. Markus and Z. Kunda. 1986. Stability and malleability of the self-concept. *Journal of Personality and Social Psychology*, 51, 858–66; D.A. Gioia, M. Schultz, and K.G. Corley. 2000. Organizational identity, image, and adaptive instability. *Academy of Management Review*, 25, 63–81.

14. Please see "Transforming 'Growing Pains' into 'Identity Gains' " in this volume.

15. D.M. Rousseau. 1998. Why workers still identify with organizations. *Journal of Organizational Behavior* 19: 217–233.

DISCERNMENT
Who is God Calling Me to Be?

I am not what happened to me, but who I choose to become.

—James Hollis

Visioning requires that we understand who we are and that we be, see, and live the vision in our thoughts and actions. We become the vision itself. Having a positive vision of the future directly affects our sense of wholeness and emotional well-being. The essays in this section introduce new ideas and take us down many paths to deepen our understanding and integrative role in this discernment process.

The Rev. Renee Miller in her essay, "A Life of Discernment," suggests that we approach discernment as a way of life rather than a prelude to choice-making. Discernment is an inclusive, all embracing exercise, and when we live into it, our lives are enriched with truth in a kind of lived prayer.

Passion, Dr. Mathew Sheep writes, is often realized when we reach beyond our own identity to embrace something greater than our selves. He connects passion, identity, and wellness for the well-functioning of the whole person.

In "Renewing Vocational Visioning," the Rev. Elizabeth Geitz, suggests that God is the Forever Pursuer, who loves, searches, and knows us and from whom we cannot hide. According to Elizabeth, the first and most important step in discernment is taking the time to notice where God is trying to reach us and letting God in.

Through the scriptures, the Rev. Canon Hartshorn Murphy writes about the intrinsic and dynamic relationship among vision, community, and God. In his essay, "Discernment through Community," he presents God's vision as one that is filtered and focused in a human context—lived into and through our fallible human lives.

The Rev. Canon Scott Hayashi takes us on a train ride to illustrate that clarity comes in fleeting moments as we live out our vision of the world. He offers practical steps to guide us in our visioning process and emphasizes the practice of helping a person to live life as a child of God, one who is on a mission to make God's vision of this world a reality.

A Life of Discernment

M. Renée Miller

He who knows others is clever; he who knows himself has discernment.

—Lao Tzu

"When will God speak to me, and tell me what to do, Rabbi?" the young man asked.

"Our God, blessed be He, is always speaking to you, if you have ears to hear," replied the Rabbi.

"I never hear a voice, Teacher," he said quietly.

"Yahweh spoke you into being as Yahweh spoke creation into being; as Yahweh spoke the covenant to Abraham; as Yahweh spoke our fathers and mothers through the wilderness," the Rabbi answered.

"But, why can't I hear?" he almost whispered.

"When your heart becomes as quiet as your whispered question, you will hear the still, small voice of God. Blessed be God."

—M. Renée Miller *Fertile Soil in a Barren Land*, 2005

Part of being human is engaging in the process of discernment. Discernment actually begins when we give voice to our longings for life in all of its fullness and it doesn't end until the fullness of life has ebbed into eternity. Life in its plentitude is always presenting us with new and different options to which we must give response. This is at once a great gift that is offered to us, and also a great challenge. The great challenge is that we will reduce discernment to nothing more than achieving a result—getting a question answered—making a choice—coming to a decision.

When we find ourselves presented with a new possibility that requires action, we immediately feel the need of a process that will assist us in weighing the risks and rewards, so that we can make a prudent and wise response. We live in fear of not knowing, and if knowing, knowing only partially. So, we go to our spiritual toolbox, unclasp the hinge, and pull out our discernment tools. We consider. We reflect. We pray. We ask for input from friends and colleagues. We look for insight and inspiration. Then, when we reach a sense of clarity or when we feel our tools can do no more for us, we make a decision and pray that our discernment was done with enough intentionality that the resulting decision will be the right one. Sometimes it is, and sometimes it isn't. Unfortunately, the discernment tools we employ are not flawless when it comes to choice making.

When used as tools alone that will result in an answer, prayer and reflection are sometimes stripped of their true purpose which is to lead us into the heart of God. Rather, it is that we have exercised discernment about the wrong thing. We've been focused on a decision, an answer, rather than making our heart so still that it is able to detect the subtle, but sublime, sounds from heaven. Discernment is not so much about choice making as it is about living attentively. It is not so much a process to employ at certain critical times, as it is something to be lived every day.

We may find ourselves thinking of discernment as little more than trying to uncover something we cannot see. It is okay. This suggests that discernment is an attribute to be cultivated rather than an action to be taken. When we approach discernment as a way to live life rather than as a prelude to choice making, there is an opportunity to continually "grasp and comprehend what is obscure." When we embrace a life of discernment we are surprised to find that the choices that need to be made throughout our lives are revealed by piecing together the unfolding moments of daily life and reflecting on the meaning of those moments as they occur. Compared to this process, periods of sporadic, episodic, focused input and evaluation are paltry, unproductive options that do not bring the fullness that steady attention to each moment brings.

When we live a life of discernment rather than simply employing a discernment process to do choice making, time becomes our ally. There is no need to hurry the discernment process. Sometimes it takes a long time—even a lifetime. In fact, discernment seems to elude us most when we are most eager for its presence. When it suspects we're aiming right for it, discernment seems to play a devilish game of hide and seek. It peeks around a corner only to disappear behind a pole when we approach too quickly, too closely.

I am not ordinarily an indecisive person. Even if I feel some uncertainty about taking a particular direction, I can usually cut through the fogginess by using the standard discernment tools from my spiritual toolbox. I talk with trusted people who have wisdom and objectivity. I read and reflect on sacred texts. I pray faithfully—even tearfully—to the One who has the power to give illumination. I examine the circumstances and situations that are a part of the decision needing to be made. And, as a last resort, I take out pen and paper to begin the ubiquitous pro and con list.

At one point in my life, however, I felt keenly that a decision needed to be made, but I couldn't seem to gain any clarity about the way forward. I pursued discernment with the trained and focused eye of the most expert photographer, ready to capture the decision the moment it came across my viewfinder. I utilized the discernment tools from my spiritual toolbox with intention and receptivity, but years went by without the decision even peeking from behind a leafy tree. The longer I searched for it with no result, the more frustrated I became. I knew a decision needed to be made, but I couldn't see what it was. I felt it was my responsibility to do the discernment (notice the use of the verb *do*) so the decision would be cajoled out from behind the leafy tree. Simply giving attention and awareness to my everyday living didn't seem to be a faithful response when I felt so certain a decision was required.

One day I was lamenting—no, complaining—to my son about the elusiveness of the decision and my frustration in the discernment process and he said, "Why don't you just keep doing what you're doing until it's time to do something else?" Ah, so there was the bigger truth. Just do what I was doing until it was time to do something else.

I began to realize that as long as I directed my discernment energy toward making a decision, I was missing living the life I had right then. The decision that I felt needed to be made would only emerge in the living of the life that I had—not in the life I imagined for myself, but one which had no edges. When my son's words descended into the dark, soft, open space of my soul, I was able to relax. It was as if I had just set ten bags of groceries on the kitchen counter and could finally sit down and breathe softly and fully. I stopped trying to ensnare a decision through the stalking techniques of discernment. Instead, I lived my life with two important intentions. First, I invited discernment into my life—to show up at dinner, at work, at prayer, at the movies, at the coffee bar, in sorrow and grief, in joy and contentment.

Secondly, I kept my eyes and heart open to notice her presence in the disparate moments of life and I tried to hear what she wanted to say to me in those moments.

In *The Alchemist* the popular writer, Paul Coelho, writes about the need to pay attention to the omens in our lives because they are often the signs that lead us to places we might not otherwise go. When it comes to discernment, such a way of being feels a little like consulting a psychic or engaging in some other nefarious necromancy. But, the word "omen" is allied to the Latin word *"audire"*—meaning, to hear. Omens are not metaphysical, new age, magical directions leading to buried treasure. Rather, they are the voice of God we can hear in the unfolding moments of our life. When we hold the moment in our mind—when we are concentrated and focused on it—we are able to hear what God might be trying to say to us. We are able to hear what God might be trying to reveal to us.

Living in the present moment has become a trendy way to think about mindfulness, a trendy way to think about living with awareness. But, the capacity for attentiveness is really about what we hold in our mind. An example of this might be how focused and concentrated we are when we know we need to pick up a loaf of bread on the way home from work. We hold the bread in our mind until we get to the store to purchase it. The Good News translation of Proverbs 4:23 says, "Be careful how you think; your life is shaped by your thoughts." The mind is limitless, and we may sometimes feel that we are hopeless and hapless victims of its whims. Mindfulness in its broader context helps us see that the power of our minds is also the power of our souls, that what we hold in our mind affects what we hold in our souls. When our mind is still, our soul can become still. When our mind is attentive and aware, our soul is attentive and aware.

The life of discernment is the way of this deeper sense of mindfulness. Clarity emerges from that life of discernment only when we hold our mind on something. When Jesus asked a blind man, "What do you want me to do for you?" (Luke 18:41) the blind man didn't need to go away to think about it, he didn't need to ask his friends what would be best, he didn't need to ask what Jesus meant, he didn't need to make a list of the pluses and minuses. He answered immediately and with clarity. He said, "Let me see again." (Luke 18:41) He was in the habit of practicing mindfulness. He held one thing in his mind—he wanted to see. And this made it possible for him to be clear in his heart and in his thoughts in the moment when he encountered Jesus.

One of the reasons that decision-making is so difficult is because we are easily caught in what I call discernment dualism. We believe that there is a right choice and a wrong choice and that we have to ferret out the right one so that the wrong one will be avoided. The very act of trying to weigh the positives and the negatives tends to lead us to making a decision that favors the side with the most positives. In truth, what may be the best decision is the one that seems to have the most negatives, because it is possible that the most long-term, life-giving, positive result may be achieved there. When we dally around in discernment dualism, we can't imagine how choosing the decision with the most negatives could ever turn out to be the best decision. When we shed our discernment dualism, letting go of the either/or tension, allowing discernment to be lived in the moments of our lives, we become less obsessed with right and wrong answers, right and wrong choices, right and wrong decisions, and become more aligned with the unfolding of life tinged with the touch of heaven.

Consider the story of Ruth. Had she been dancing with discernment dualism, she would probably never have left her country of Moab to follow her mother-in-law Naomi into Bethlehem. The only "positive"' on Ruth's list for going with Naomi was that she loved and trusted her. The "negative" list was much more detailed. To follow Naomi, Ruth would have to leave her family, leave her faith, live among a people and culture that was unfamiliar and foreign to her, take on responsibility not only for herself but for Naomi as well. In other words, she had to choose to abandon the life she had, knowing she would probably never return to it.

By staying focused on the potential of the moment rather than on the past or the future, she was able to make a decision that allowed potential to flourish. God had more in mind for Ruth than she could ever have imagined. Certainly, God was abundantly able to transform the negatives into positives. This is the revelation that is as real as our own name. God always has more in mind for us than we can imagine, more than we would ever believe is possible, more than we could ever hope for or anticipate. The way to discover that "more" is to stand on that razor edge between the past and the future. It is to see what this moment is trying to tell us. The negatives are often vestiges of the past, and the positives are often our hopes for the future, but we have no certainty that what we believe to be a positive will remain so, or that a negative won't be transformed into something fulfilling beyond our wildest dreams.

This makes discernment a much more inclusive, all-embracing exercise than we might like it to be. It's much more manageable as an activity that we take out of our spiritual toolbox when we're at a point of choice making. Living with discernment as a familiar, ever-present companion requires attention, awareness, hearing, reflection, processing, then more reflection, hearing, reflection, processing . . . It's counterintuitive because it's a lived prayer that is always slightly messy, but nonetheless leads us into a depth of being we could not have reached by relying only on the items in our toolbox. In this entwined relationship with discernment, the moments of our lives become full and potent. It is the way we hear in those moments, the voice of heaven calling us to re-direct ourselves, to re-imagine a way of being in the world, to re-new an older pattern in life, to re-lease an unhealthy habit. Ultimately, a life of discernment is a life of trust and it is most surely the way we incarnate the words from Proverbs: "It is your own face that you see reflected in the water; it is your own self that you see in your heart." (Proverbs 27:19) When our souls are brought into that place of stillness through a life of discernment, clarity and truth shine as clear as a full moon on a starless night.

The Quest for Passion, Creativity, and Wholeness

Mathew L. Sheep

> *There is no passion to be found playing small—in settling for a life that is less than the one you are capable of living.*
>
> —Nelson Mandela

> *If you want to build a ship, don't drum up people to collect wood and don't assign them tasks and work, but rather teach them to long for the endless immensity of the sea.*
>
> —Antoine de Saint-Exupéry

Most of us would agree that the obligation to complete a set of assigned tasks or goals—to collect wood and build a boat—is not on a par motivationally with a deeper yearning, a passionate quest for the "immensity of the sea"—the tantalizing yearning to experience the sublime, the endless ocean, untamable in its ever-changing moods. Yet somehow, as we go through life, the grander images and narratives become obscured by the mundane steps and procedures they involve—the ends being swallowed up in the means.

I understand this. Most of my life has been spent on or around the water. Growing up along the Outer Banks of North Carolina, I loved boating and swimming, and I could hardly bear the wait until my dad deemed me old enough to buy my first surfboard. Later in life, as a Coast Guard officer, I remained in awe that the sea could change from placid aquamarine mirror to raging dark monster, or back again—all in a matter of hours or even minutes. The sea was and is my passion (notwithstanding my current residence in Illinois). My love is not for sailboats or surfboards, per se. They can only take me there—to the unfettered horizon where water touches sky, to the crest of the ride of my life, to a world of unfathomable beauty that ebbs and flows with the subtle colors of life. All is not safe, comfortable, or predictable in that world—far from it—but it excites my being (and well-being) every time I am in its presence and inspires wonder at what new experiences in life could be possible.[1]

The sea is one of my passions. I have others more foundational—God, family, friends, research, music. What are your passions? And what does it actually mean to say that we are passionate about life or toward certain aspects of life? What difference does passion make in our thinking, emotions, attitudes, choices, performance, and creativity? How do passion and creativity impact our wholeness and wellness, as well as the wellness of others—the individuals and collectivities with whom our lives are intertwined?

What is passion? It can mean many things, but is often associated with "desires, behaviors, and thoughts that suggest urges with considerable force."[2] Hence, passion is often associated with romantic love or strong emotion. Its origin as a word goes back to the passion of Christ as he was crucified (from the Latin *passio*, or suffering). Passion can also be more clearly understood and enacted in one's life in terms of its relationship to identity and motivation.

Passion and Identity: "Is This Really Who I Am?"

To do anything in life with *passion*—pursuing one's dream, discerning a vocation, investing oneself in an academic degree, growing a family, contributing one's talents toward a cause, or even engaging in leisure activities or hobbies—almost seems equivalent to doing those things in life that resonate most harmoniously with one's sense of self—identity. For example, it would seem nonsensical to say, "Well, I'm *passionate* about playing the piano (or writing short stories, or playing tennis), but it's *not really me*." Intuitively, we know that we are passionate about certain activities *precisely* because they fulfill our sense of self—our self-identity— whether actual or aspirational (the self that we want to become). We may also be passionate about certain activities and goals because we perceive that they develop relationships that we believe are important to who we are—our social identities—and thus further our priorities of aspirations, beliefs, and values.

Indeed, one definition emphasizes that a "defining characteristic of passion is that the passionate activity has been *internalized in the person's identity* [italics mine]."[3] Thus, passion goes beyond mere engagement in *what* we are doing and *where* we are doing it, to be seen as an integral, perhaps necessary, part of *who we are*.[4]

For example, classical musicians can endure—even thrive on—long and grueling daily practice sessions not only because they are passionate about the interpretation and performance of music, but also because they are engaged in an activity that fulfills and develops their identity—"I am (or want to become) a virtuoso musician. That is not only what I do; it is part of who I am." When the streams of identity and action converge, the confluence is the swirling and beautiful river we call Passion.

It could well be said that the difference between a job and a discerned calling is the element of passion where one's work and identity are not only congruent, but mutually energizing (synergistic). Taking it a step further, passion is often realized when we reach beyond our own identity to embrace something greater than ourselves. One of the most powerful forces that both lures and drives a human life forward is a deep, spiritual yearning to transcend the self, or at least narrow self-absorption. The quest for passion is a search for some seemingly elusive "spark" that transforms life into a daily adventure populated with meaningful relationships and inspired by a purpose.

For example, the Apostle Paul commended the Christians in Thessalonica for their "labor prompted by love." (1 Thessalonians 1:3, NIV) Likewise, it could be said that a certain portion of our life's energy is directed toward the search for an unpretentious labor of love—work energized and sustained by a deeply held passion for its nature and purpose—something we may do "heartily (from the soul)." (Colossians 3:23, Amplified Bible)

As we scan our social networks and relationships for some super-ordinate goal, our reason for doing and being, that reason may come in the form of a cause, calling, purpose, or person that might engender the long-sought spark of passion. Our passionate engagement in acts of ministry enables us to transcend ourselves in a way that, paradoxically, enables us to realize our authentic selves. Whether we are passionate about working toward the realization of the Millennium Development Goals, realizing the promise and hope of "Ubuntu"[5] as our interdependent identity in Christian community as well as in the world, or whatever we find to be the compelling purpose of our time, we lose our self-interest in favor of connection with a greater whole—a purpose much greater than ourselves in connection with others. Such a connection can infuse our work with meaning and creative potential.

Passion and Meaningfulness: *Why Do I Do What I Do?*

George Carlin once said, "Life is not measured by the number of breaths we take, but by the moments that take our breath away." What really takes your breath away? What charges your batteries and causes your life juices to start flowing? Even if the answers to these questions are not intertwined harmoniously with your daily life, there is much that can be done to integrate life and work so that they are both passionate pursuits and authentic expressions of your identity.

One view of passion is in its relation to human motivation. In Western cultures, theories of motivation have traditionally treated human desire as driven by a relatively superficial and self-interested (though perhaps very real) lack of something—e.g., basic necessities, safety, achievement, affiliation, and power. Lack, or the perception of a gap between one's desired and actual condition, causes an uncomfortable tension in our lives that spurs relentless efforts to reduce the lack.[6] Work, no matter how mundane or repetitive, becomes the means to reduce such tension by satisfying our lacks—or desires.

Downside of Traditional View

The downside of this traditional view of motivation is that meaningfulness gets lost in the shuffle. As one social scientist put it, "Discourses around motivation appear when work no longer fulfills or satisfies."[7] In other words, when meaningfulness is not found in one's work, then more mundane and externally oriented forms of motivation (such as reward and punishment) have become "surrogates for the search for meaning."[8]

These contemporary assumptions about desire and motivation have been effective in controlling worker performance through incentive packages that motivate; however, they have a dark side, as well. The very notion of "desire as lack" signals a deeper cultural problem with the nature of work itself—viewing it only as a self-interested end rather than as an other-directed means to realize one's deepest-held beliefs about meaningfulness in life.[9] A passionate view of our life's work emphasizes the latter—re-infusing work with meaning that energizes and inspires us to approach work as something more.

In my own life's journey, I discovered much later than I would have liked that life is not just about trying to become less selfish. That perspective alone can be seen as a negative or pathological view of "fixing what's wrong." Rather, from a positive perspective, life is also about "strengthening what is right," and that can mostly be summed up in one word: contribution. As an academic, that point is constantly drilled into my consciousness in the peer review process for academic publications. The one question that must be compellingly answered in research articles is: "What is the contribution?" How does this study contribute in new ways to our knowledge of theory and improvement of practice? To those who are somewhat philosophical (like me), it is not hard to see that this question applies to life just as well as to research articles. *Life is about contribution*, and that's really about it. What are we creating? What will we leave behind? We are eager to re-imagine what work itself is all about, and we are not fearful of asking the hard questions: What do I really consider to be the ultimate cause and purpose of my existence? And what does my labor of love have to do with that?

However, a brief word of caution: passion is like any other energy. It may be exercised helpfully or hurtfully; it may enhance or harm one's sense of well-being. It may be an igniting spark or a debilitating obsession. How can we know the difference?

Harmony Versus Obsession: Is Passion Always Healthy?

Passion is not always a good thing. We all know that the word passion can be used in a less desirable sense—e.g., "crimes of passion." Social science can help us discern the difference between healthy versus unhealthy passion. Human passion can be either harmonious or obsessive. Harmonious passion can actually increase our sense of well-being and performance, while obsessive passion can destroy them.[10] The reason for this is that harmonious passion is under our self-control and allows us to engage in a variety of activities for a well-rounded life. Harmonious passion does not absorb or overtake a person's identity but is instead well-integrated with it.[11] By contrast, obsessive passion results in compulsive behavior not under the control of will and reason, and it thus dominates uncontrollably the life and identity of the one who holds it.[12]

For the ultimate example of a life lived in harmonious passion, we need look no further than the life of Jesus Christ—transparently passionate (to the point of overturning tables in the Temple), ultimately sacrificial (as the very word "passion" is derived from Christ's crucifixion), and the epitome of rationality (the Pharisees had no comeback for his logic) and openness (to little children, adulterers, and tax collectors). Jesus certainly had a clear sense of his identity and that identity was inseparable from the work he came to do. Thus, we see that passion is not the direct opposite of rationality. Instead, healthy passion is a controlled, integrated energy that helpfully enables rather than hurtfully overpowers human activity and relationships.

Creativity and Performance:
What Difference Does Passion Make?

Without passion, man is a mere latent force and possibility, like the flint which awaits the shock of the iron before it can give forth its spark.

—Henri Frederic Amiel
(Swiss philosopher, 1821–1881)

What difference does passion make to creative outcomes? I suggest the following illustration:

Imagine that two virtuoso pianists individually, consecutively play the same musical composition to the same audience. They each strike the same notes with nearly identical meter and force, and they complete the piece in the same amount of time. Yet, the performance of one of the pianists creates a high energy and passion to the point of joyful tears in both musician and hearers, while the other performance is just deemed as technically correct. Musicians might describe the passionate performance as having the right "vibe." Entertainers and critics alike might call such performances "magical" or "electrifying."

Similarly, two people work in the same area at an identical task. However, one simply goes about the required processes in a methodically proper fashion with little personal investment in or satisfaction from the work, while the other experiences "flow" as self and work become one and as time passes unnoticed (Csikszentmihalyi, 1990). We could go on, describing how authors and artists talk of being inspired by their "muse"; friends and lovers speak of perfect "chemistry" in interpersonal relationships; sports teams account victory not only to their technical performances but to their team "spirit."[13]

What may be the most powerful explanation for these stark contrasts between the mundane and the exceptional? Passion! Passion and its transmission to others can make all the difference in the creative outcomes of almost any vocational performance. If people are passionate about an activity, then their motivation to do it well comes from deep within.

Passion and Wholeness/Wellness

As psychologists and theologians alike have been telling us for years, our mental and emotional wellness is linked to our ability to put the pieces of our lives together in a coherent, integrated whole that makes sense to us in our self-concept.[14] We have seen in this chapter how passion is related to our identity as well as creative outcomes. Moreover, we saw that harmonious passion can increase our subjective well-being and quality of performance. Passionate endeavors are much more likely to produce a state of "flow"—the focused engagement of the "whole person" in a task, in which self and work become one and time passes unnoticed. Passion and flow have been linked to creative action and innovative outcomes.[15] To visually summarize all of this, the chart below traces the process by which passion can result in higher levels of subjective well-being.[16] Passion, identity, creativity, and holistic wellness are indeed as interdependent as the roots, trunk, leaves, and fruit of a towering tree—all of the parts are needed for the well functioning of the whole and its contribution to larger collectivities (e.g., forests and societies).

A Path Model of Passion to Well-Being

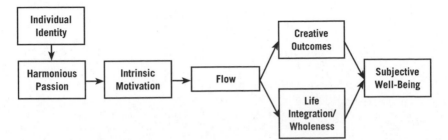

In closing, let me offer a very practical description of passionate people and why they are so often a benefit to congregations and all sorts of organizations, especially those navigating the waters of change. Research on the personality traits of passionate people showed that they like win-win solutions, handle change well, and embrace the new and different in their work. Passionate people enjoy a variety of interests and types of people, are adaptive and innovative, and are able to communicate enthusiasm without losing sight of overall goals. As one researcher put it, passionate people "like to sample a lot of different tastes from life's menu."[17]

Is it any wonder, then, that we usually enjoy being around passionate people—those who set their eyes on the immensity of the sea so that the collecting of wood takes on meaning, purpose, and joy? Is all this too lofty to attain? How can we live more moments in passionate pursuit of that which takes our breath away? How will we and our world be made better and more whole if we do?

ᕮᗢᕤ

Notes

1. For a more humorous view of this notion, read *McElligott's Pool* by Dr. Seuss.

2. A. Bennet. 2005. Exploring aspects of knowledge management that contribute to the passion expressed by its thought leaders. [Dissertation, Fielding Graduate Institute] 43–62.

3. C.E. Amiot, R.J. Vallerand, and C.M. Blanchard. 2006. Passion and psychological adjustment: A test of the person-environment fit hypothesis. *Personality and Social Psychology Bulletin* 32(2): 220–229.

4. E. Gubman. 2004. From engagement to passion for work: The search for the missing person. *Human Resource Planning* 27(3): 42–46.

5. For a discussion of this term, please see "Toward a Theology of Identity" by The Very Rev. Canon Michael J. Battle, Ph.D in this volume.

6. The classic Maslow's hierarchy of needs, Herzberg's two-factor theory, McClelland's three-needs theory, and others serve as examples of traditional needs-based theories of motivation.

7. S. Linstead and J. Brewis. 2007. Passion, knowledge and motivation: Ontologies of desire. *Organization* 14(3): 351–371.

8. B. Sievers. 1986. Beyond the surrogate of motivation. *Organization Studies* 7(4): 335–351.

9. i.e., what one contributes to benefit some greater whole or what one deems to be life's ultimate meaning and purpose.

10. R.J. Vallerand, S. Salvy, G.A. Mageau, A.J. Elliot, P.L. Denis, F.M.E. Grouzet, and C. Blanchard. 2007. On the role of passion in performance. *Journal of Personality* 75(3): 505–534.

11. Ibid.

12. In other words, passions are not automatically beneficial or positive in nature. Destructive passions, such as greed, inappropriate lust, anger, and so on, seem to be more a matter of carrying an otherwise healthy passion to the degree of obsessive attitude or behavior beyond their more benign form (of harmonious passions). There is even Biblical

allusion to this view of passions. For example, greed can be an abusive obsession with making money, but few are likely to argue that making money is an evil in itself. (1 Timothy 6:10) Admiration of beauty may turn into obsessive lust (e.g., David and Bathsheba). Anger is treated as an inevitable response at times, but it becomes destructive when one ruminates on it obsessively into the next day (Ephesians 4:26).

13. M.L. Sheep and P.O. Foreman. 2007. A marriage made in heaven? Exploring the relationships of organizational identity and spirituality. Paper presented at the 67th Annual Academy of Management Meeting, Philadelphia.

14. E.H. Erikson, *Insight and responsibility: Lectures on the Ethical Implications of Psychoanalytic Insight* (New York W. W. Norton & Company, Inc. 1964).

15. "Flow" refers to a totally involving work experience that is sustained by stimuli in the activity itself. M. Csikszentmihaly, *Flow: The Psychology of Optimal Experience* (New York: Harper & Row, Publishers, 1990). C. Belitz and M. Lundstrom. *The Power of Flow* (New York: Harmony Books, 1997).

16. Also see CREDO Institute, Inc. 2006. *Episcopal Clergy Wellness: A Report to the Church on the State of Clergy Wellness.*

17. E. Gubman. 2004. From engagement to passion for work: The search for the missing person. *Human Resource Planning* 27(3): 42–46.

Renewing Vocational Vision

Elizabeth Geitz

"We're here because, we're here because, we're here because we're here."
These familiar camp song lyrics, sung to the tune of "Auld Lang Syne,"
were a childhood favorite of mine. I often belted them out at the top of
my lungs for no apparent reason, driving my parents to distraction. Now
as a parent myself, I can understand why. If we're just "here because,
we're here because we're here," then why have so many of us spent so
many years trying to figure out who we are and why we're here? No, we
can't simply be here because we're here.

If not, then why and for what did God create us? What are people for
anyway? According to Judeo-Christian history, people are for relationship with God and with one another. We exist for co-existence. The purpose of our being is to "be with." In Biblical tradition to "be" is to "be
with" first God and then others.

In *The Story of Evangelism*, Robert Tuttle speaks eloquently of God
as the first evangelist, God as the Forever Pursuer, God as the One who
never stops pursuing you and me because God yearns for relationship
with us.[1] Throughout scripture, regardless of what people do, God never
stops loving them and wanting to be in relationship with them.

The psalmist tells us, "O LORD you have searched me out and known
me. You know my sitting down and my rising up; you discern my thoughts
from afar . . . you press upon me behind and before and lay your hand upon
me . . . Where can I go then from your Spirit? Where can I flee from your
presence?" Nowhere, the psalmist tells us. Nowhere. (Psalm 139:1, 4, 6)

First and foremost we are meant to be in relationship with our Creator,
the Forever Pursuer, who loves us with a love that knows no bounds, who
searches us and knows us, and from whom we cannot flee no matter how
fervently we sometimes try. And this is where Christian discernment and
vocational renewal begin—in a one-to-one relationship with our loving
Creator. Renewing vocational vision begins with this essential, foundational relationship. It begins with us and God.

I'll always remember my first silent retreat. We traveled to a convent for the weekend and were told that as soon as Friday night dinner was over we could not talk until after breakfast on Sunday. My face obviously reflected the fear I felt because my priest turned to me and said, "Yep, Elizabeth, it's just you and God," whereupon everyone laughed.

So, I now share this wisdom with you, "It's just you and God." Bask in that for a moment; reflect on the sheer simplicity and beauty of it. Invite God into your life, not just in the quiet moments or times of trouble, but invite God to join with you in moments of joy and celebration. What do you enjoy doing most? Invite God into that experience. Just spend some time together, whenever and wherever it works for you.

If you're an extrovert, you may need to walk, ride a bike, or, yes, dance! However you let God into your life is how God wants to be with you. The Forever Pursuer will not say, "No, no, no, that doesn't quite suit me; let's do this instead!"

In his book, *The Word is Very Near You*, Martin Smith writes of a "radical revisioning of the whole enterprise of prayer," in which he shares his belief that, while prayer is a conversation between us and God, it is not a conversation we start.[2] God initiates the conversation of prayer, not us. If we see something in nature that speaks to us of our Creator, that's God's way of initiating a conversation with us. If we feel called to pray for someone in need or a friend who is ill, Smith reminds us that "God is already in the situation of need . . . God has reached out to us from that place and touched off a spark of response to that need . . . God then recruits our love and concern."[3]

God as Forever Pursuer. God as Initiator. Our role is simply to be open, to intuit and then respond to that invitation. That's all: it's easy!

But it isn't, is it? If it were, we would be in an almost constant state of communion with God. Discernment would be a snap. What bliss! What wonder! How enriched our lives would be! No, it isn't that easy. There are a number of reasons for that; I'd like to mention two.

First, to be in a relationship at any level other than a superficial one requires intimacy, and intimacy is scary. As much as we desire it, we fear intimacy, whether in our relationships with one another or with God. Paradoxically, we run away from the very thing we most desire. I have found that simply being honest with God and naming the fear can begin to open doors.

In addition, for any relationship to thrive it must be based on honesty. When we are upset with somebody, angry, or deeply hurt, our relationship is not what it could be or what God intends it to be. Similarly, when we feel that God has failed us, has not kept our loved ones from harm, or has allowed them to get sick or die, we may not feel like being in relationship with God at that moment. I, for one, can put up all kinds of roadblocks when this occurs and my excuses for not praying start multiplying—"I'm too busy," or even better, "I'm too busy doing God's work," or "I plan to go on retreat soon and make up for lost time," or "Just as soon as this big issue is resolved," or "Fill in the blanks." When we feel this way we need to own it and be honest with God about it.

Taking time to notice where God is trying to reach you and letting God in is the first and most important step you can take when seeking to renew your vocational vision. The second is to trust, trust, trust.

"I know the plans I have for you," declares the Lord, "plans to prosper you and not to harm you, plans to give you hope and a future." (Jeremiah 29:11) These words from the prophet Jeremiah are on my desk, written on a postcard perched on a little stand. As my spiritual journey has unfolded with many twists, turns, and dead ends along the way, I have often reflected on these words. On more than one occasion, I have impatiently beseeched God, "Okay, you may know the plans, but I don't know the plans. So, what are they?"

Discernment about what God is calling you to do is a lifelong process, with your vocation regularly in need of revision and renewal. While the process is centered in you and God, it is enveloped in the arms of a loving Christian community. No one can be objective about themselves. What you think is God's voice may in fact be your own or one of the many other voices in your life. Reaching out to people you trust on a regular basis, and faithfully listening to them, is also key. The faithful Christian asks over and over again, "What is it that God really wants me to do with my life at this time and in this place?" There is no question more vexing or perplexing.

As an active layperson, before attending seminary, this was a question I struggled with and at times stumbled over. Why? Because when mainline denominations started teaching about lay ministry I believed what I was taught. Yet when I tried to be a lay minister in the church I found it difficult with unexpected obstacles. In the Episcopal Church, the shift in emphasis towards lay ministry began with the 1979 Book of Common Prayer in which the catechism articulates four orders of ministry. Nonetheless a generation later, the church is just beginning to live into that change. How often I have heard that ministry begins with baptism, but seldom did I feel validated in that ministry. What I did not realize at the time was that much of what I was already doing was ministry—at home, at work, and in the church. I just didn't recognize it for what it truly was—ministry in the name of Christ on behalf of the people of God.

It is important to claim the ministry you're already involved in, because *authentic ministry occurs wherever and whenever you are using the gifts God has given you for the common good.* Wherever and whenever—whether it's at home, at work, at school, at church, or even when you're on vacation—that's where ministry takes place.

What lies at the heart of ministry in these various settings is your use of the gifts God has given you, along with the passion God has placed in your heart. It is helpful to distinguish here between gifts and skills. Skills are attributes learned and developed over the years at which you may be quite competent, but which may or may not feed you. Over time, if you are using only your skills and not your gifts, you can begin to feel burned out, in need of replenishment. You might want to spend some time discerning whether your current vocational reality primarily utilizes your gifts or your skills. If it is predominantly skill-based and you are feeling drained or depleted much of the time, it may be helpful to focus on your God-given gifts that nurture you in a different way.

Take a moment to reflect on a time in your life when you reached out to someone else. Let a memory rise to the surface that is particularly meaningful. What gift did you use, not what skill, but what gift? As you reflect on this gift in light of your vocation, you might want to ponder these words written by Sam Keen in *The Passionate Life: Stages of Loving.*

> We are each called by name. A small voice, easily ignored, whispers: "This is your work. This is your place. These are your neighbors. This is your mate. This is the burden you are to bear. This is the healing you are to undertake. This is the gift you are to exercise. These are the wounds you must suffer. This is the arena in which you must act the drama of your life."[4]

Now let's explore a little. Maybe you've been involved in the same ministries for so long that you can't imagine doing anything else. To begin to get in touch with some of your hidden or not-yet-developed gifts requires imagination.

Imagination lies at the heart of every creative idea. Unless you are willing to let your imagination run free, unless you are willing to break old paradigms and molds, creativity will be stifled and much will be lost. For that reason, imagination lies at the heart of every scientific and technological advance that moves civilization to a new realm. Imagination also lies at the heart of the Judeo-Christian tradition.

Where would all of us be right now if Moses had not had imagination? In his book, *Prophetic Imagination*, Walter Brueggemann stresses the radical break made by Moses with "the social reality of Pharaoh's Egypt."[5] Moses, born as a slave, calls upon the one true God, Yahweh, who delivers the people from the hands of the Egyptians. Without prophetic imagination, Moses would never have been able to bring forth in Israel an alternative consciousness, and that is part of the task of ministry—to nurture and evoke a consciousness that is different from the prevailing culture.[6]

A prophetic imagination dares to envision a world based on the life and teachings of Jesus Christ, enabling us truly to love one another, just as Jesus loves us, enabling us not only to receive the Holy Spirit, but to allow ourselves to be transformed by her. Imagine such a world. How radically different it would be.

How can you have enough freedom to imagine and embrace a renewed vocational vision? To do so, you need to ask not whether the vision is practical, but whether it can be imagined. You need to ask if you have been so co-opted by the secular world that you "have been robbed of the courage or power to think an alternative thought."[7] Moreover, in today's image-driven culture, you can be gradually robbed of your own imagination by those who project their images onto you, filling your head and heart with them until you begin to believe them yourself. As you renew and revitalize your vocational calling, you do not need to ask if a particular vision can be implemented, but whether or not the vision can be imagined and whether it is truly your own or someone else's vision of you.

Several years ago our family visited Disney World, which is more filled with imagination than any place I've ever been. Before one show, we saw a short movie about imagination and the possibilities it brings. There were signs posted all around that said, "Imagination is better than knowledge. Imagination is your key to life's coming attractions." I would add, "Imagination is your key to vital, vibrant vocational renewal."

As I write this essay, I am preparing to embark on a pilgrimage to Cameroon, Africa, to The Good Shepherd Home for Children, a home for fifty AIDS orphans on a remote mountain in Bamenda. Since viewing a *Today* show special over thirty years ago featuring Miss Lillian Carter working in an African village, part of me has known that someday God would lead me to a similar place. During the special, Miss Lillian shared a picture of herself on a motorcycle surrounded by the village children. I often told people that someday I would be in just such a picture, minus the motorcycle! Now I will be and I am ready. Nonetheless, answering God's leading in my life with a resounding "yes" feels like my first jump from the high dive. Venturing from the known to the unknown, encountering a different culture with unfamiliar customs challenges me to the very core of my being.

What makes such a leap possible is that one-on-one never-failing relationship with the God who has searched me out and from whom I have never been able to flee, regardless of how hard I have sometimes tried. What makes it possible is ongoing, trusting relationships with the people of God, and trusting that my Creator is already present in this, and every new vocational endeavor. God is already there, beckoning me to join in. It's only "new" to me. What makes it possible is the imagination to envision using the gifts God has so graciously given in unexpected, unexplored ways.

My prayer is that you will let your imagination run free as you join in what God is already doing—enabling you to live into and claim your own renewed vocational vision. Enjoy the journey!

☙❧

Notes

1. Robert G. Tuttle, *The Story of Evangelism: A History of the Witness to the Gospel* (Nashville: Abingdon Press, 2006), 4.

2. Martin L. Smith, *The Word is Very Near You: A Guide to Praying with Scripture* (Lanham, MD: Cowley Publications, 1989), 19.

3. Ibid., 22

4. Sam Keen, *The Passionate Life: Stages of Loving* (San Francisco: HarperSan Francisco, 1983), 171.

5. Walter Brueggemann, *The Prophetic Imagination* (Philadelphia: Fortress Press, 1978), 15.

6. Ibid., 13, as discussed in Douglas Hall, *Lighten Our Darkness* (Philadelphia: Westminster Press, 1976).

7. Ibid., 44.

Discernment through Community

Hartshorn Murphy, Jr.

Without vision, the people perish . . .

(Proverbs 29:18)

The editor of the Book of Proverbs, a series of self-evident, common sense truths (sometimes called "mother's wit"), describes vision as being so essential that without it, the people would die. The New Revised Standard Version renders this passage: "Where there is no prophecy, the people cast off restraint." A community without a common direction and purpose runs amok, without either borders or boundaries, without the ability to say "no" to every challenge and opportunity in ministry. God's people—without a shared vision—become distracted, dissipated, and dispirited.

But what do we mean, precisely, by "vision"? To be a visionary is to see that which is not yet.

Examples abound in religious tradition.

In the Hebrew Scriptures, there is the story of Abram, whom some account as the father of monotheism. Abram receives a call to leave his home in Haran for Canaan and, although married to a ninety-year-old post-menopausal woman called to, at age 100, father a new nation whose descendants will be "like the stars." (Genesis 12) In a land not his own, God projected for Abram a vision of a future that was, by Abram's faithfulness to it, taking root in the present. Abram receives a new name (Abraham) and a new destiny.

Moses, an abandoned child and haunted (and hunted) murderer, receives a revelation that he is to lead the descendants of Abraham from slavery to freedom, to claim Canaan at last. The dream will not be denied or delayed. But Moses resisted the vision: "I am slow of speech and slow of tongue." (Exodus 4:10) How could he be an ambassador of a vision from God? But through God's promptings—and the support of his brother Aaron—Moses persists and prevails.

Finally, Ezekiel the prophet in Babylonian exile, mourning the destruction of Solomon's Temple and people, has a vision of the dead restored;

73

dry bones alive again. Judea will be resurrected and a new temple built to *tabernacle* God. (Ezekiel 37:1–14)

In the Christian Scriptures, there is the story of Saul the bounty hunter who, struck blind on the road to Damascus on his way to arrest Christians, is transformed from persecutor to proclaimer of Christ, his zeal re-directed and re-focused by a vision. (Acts 9:4)

On the penal isle of Patmos, John has a vocation as a visionary who is given to see a future in which Roman cruelty is no more and to joyfully proclaim the coming of a new heaven and a new earth which he will never live to see. (Revelations 21:1–4)

For Christians, the central visionary figure is the Christ.

Jesus, newly baptized, is driven into the desert by God's spirit to be exposed to three alternative paths by which he could live into the vocation of being a vision-caster of the Kingdom of God. (Matthew 4) The first path, symbolized by bread, was to be a populist leader of the peasant majority by meeting their physical needs. The second, symbolized by a temptation to misuse supernatural power, was to garner the people's loyalty through superstition and magic. The third, symbolized by political power, was to command through royal edict and the might of armies, human compliance with God's will. All were viable, if deeply flawed, strategies. But to choose any of them would be to choose the merely good over the best. The power of evil is the power of seduction. Satan withdraws until a "more opportune time" (Mark 4:13) for these temptations are not transitory but are archetypal—they will occur again and again, e.g. "Let the Messiah, the King of Israel, come down from the cross now, so that we may see and believe." (Mark 15:32)

All six stories—three from the Hebrew Scriptures and three from the Christian Scriptures—are stories of a God-given vision for the future.

George Barna in his book, *"The Power of Vision,"* more narrowly defines vision in this way: "Vision for ministry is a clear mental image of a preferable future imparted by God to His chosen servants and is based upon an accurate understanding of God, self, and circumstances."[1]

Barna makes clear that a vision comes as an image of the future that God prefers for the people of God. But even so, that vision is filtered and focused in a human context, lived into through fallible, human lives. Vision is thus the hilltop on the other side of the mountain on which we stand. Vision is destination, neither an itinerary nor a mission statement.

In the 1980s, Commissions on the Ministry described the candidates they sought for the priesthood with a word new to the ordained ministry: entrepreneur. The adoption of a word associated with the world of business and commerce tried to get at vision through a backdoor.

The entrepreneur priest would be a "self-starter." One who would be, to use family systems language, self-differentiated and who would be a leader capable of renewing static or declining churches, even if that meant making difficult or unpopular choices. By sheer strength of personality and persuasiveness, renewal would come. To be such a leader necessitated the development of long-range strategic plans and comprehensive mission statements, and lots of newsprint.

As a diocesan executive, I noticed that these mission statements seemed a bit, well, generic. Indeed, they could well be described as "interchangeable." All churches share the task of honoring God, proclaiming the gospel, and serving people. There was a lack of "grounding in context" to statements that failed to guide decisions about saying "yes" to some things, but more importantly, saying "no" to many others. We cannot be, in fact, all things to all people.

The idea of an entrepreneur priest represented an effort to narrow the search for candidates with a certain style and presence of clerical leadership. Strategic plans sought to create a consensus among lay leadership around the mission or purpose of the institution, however generic. But they never generated much energy or passion. They all seemed a bit fraudulent because the language and models were borrowed from the world of the marketplace rather than the world of the spirit. These descriptors of the path to be traveled (and even of the nature of the guide to lead us along the path) simply did not articulate where the road leads. Not a few judicious lay leaders would ask: "Now just why are we doing this?"

Sailors say that without a destination, every wind is a fair wind. Hikers tell us that if you don't know where you're going, any road will take you there. A vision statement—the future God yearns for this congregation in its particular context—must precede and shape both the strategic plan as well as the nature (skills, passions, and personality) of the designated leader (clergy or lay) to take us there.

At times, incompatibility emerges between leader and destiny.

The first parish I served in the early 1970s was in an increasingly impoverished African-American neighborhood in Baltimore. I was the first black priest to serve this mostly white middle-class congregation, for an internship, which would last two years. Part of the parish's personal story and collective memory was about the missed opportunity some ten years earlier when the parish had the opportunity to call an African-American as Rector but opted for the "safe" (comfortable) choice of a white priest.

Looking back, they realized that it had been a decisive moment. Had their vision been clear and compelling—to reach the residents of the neighborhood in which they were situated—they would have made a less comfortable—but more faithful—choice: selecting a rector with the background to reach the community they sought not just to serve but to evangelize. They would have initiated a heroic journey together. In many changing neighborhoods our congregations serve, the lack of a vision for the future God's wants could fairly be described as circling the wagons until the folks who look, sound, and worship like us return. But a vision for the future allows us to make the faithful choice of letting go of whatever, and whoever, does not move us along the path to reaching that place.

Where there is no vision, no sense of what God wants to do in and through us, people lose heart for ministry. As archdeacon, I once "instituted" a new vicar in a mission congregation. The gathered congregation, having completed what they thought was a faithful search for their new leader, was excited and hopeful about their future.

During his first service, the new vicar stood to make his remarks, beginning with an astounding statement: "I have no vision for this congregation. I am here, as your priest, to support you in your vision for the future." Seated behind him on the platform of the altar, I could hear an almost audible sigh of disappointment and saw more than a few heads drop in dejection.

We know what this well-meaning cleric was trying to say. But had he said it another way: "I come with no agenda but to discern, with you, God's will for this place. I know, and you know in your hearts, that God has a mighty plan for our future and together, we are called to work, pray, and give in order to attain it. And I am excited about journeying with you!" it would have changed everything; for visions are, by their nature, compelling and energizing. They give a reason to get involved; a reason to live.

Regardless of the spiritual practice we choose, spiritual directors suggest that in order to make progress on the path, we should commit to allocating one hour a day, one weekend a month, and one week each year to our practice.

Depleted and burned-out from twenty-five years of ordained ministry, I made my way like a refugee to the Mt. Calvary Monastery in Santa Barbara. It was a gracious house where the Order of the Holy Cross brothers were always welcoming. I was free to participate in the worship life of the community or not, as I wished. Nonetheless, it was plainly a place for contemplation and for prayer.

I noticed the rector of the largest parish in our diocese at meals, but it was clear that he was there for silence and solitude. The third day, as we were both preparing to return to the complexities and challenges of parish ministry, I was surprised when my colleague told me that it was his practice to go on a silent retreat three days every month for refreshment and renewal and to reconnect with his vision for his parish and himself.

The image that came to me, as I crawled home amidst a soul-crushing traffic jam on the freeway, was one of a general surveying the progress of a battle from a hillside. Unless one withdraws from the fray to take a broader view, one can easily lose sight of the goal. As I drove home, I was left to ponder this question: How is it that the pastor of our largest and busiest parish can make space in his life and ministry for this commitment? I discovered that he has always carved out this space, making it a non-negotiable prerequisite of his contract. How could he do this, and I could not? And soberingly, how much longer could I continue on this path before my well would be sucking sand; the living water, nourished by vision, long since drained away?

Much of the preceding speaks about vision in the context of congregational life. There is an assumption that God's revelation is for the People of God and the role we as lay and clergy leaders will play in moving toward that vision. That was certainly true of the biblical examples cited earlier. Each of those men were called forth for a particular ministry for their communities: Moses to lead a march to freedom; Jesus to preach hope and to die and live again for it.

Is it possible for an individual to have a personal vision apart from their community? In many cultures, the answer is yes. Native American spirituality calls for young men—and to a lesser degree, young women—to leave their tribes on a vision quest, during which the individual seeks a spiritual direction for the future. Through a variety of spiritual disciplines—sensory and sleep deprivation, fasting, long walks in monotonous landscapes—a young warrior, aided by an animal guide, seeks an inner revelation, which will give meaning and direction to life.

In Celtic spirituality, we find the tradition of "thin places" in which the individual makes pilgrimage to a holy site and there patiently awaits a vision of the eternal. Such transitory mystical experiences reconfirm a sense of God imminent as well as transcendent and sustaining the individual in the spiritual journey through life.

For one who worships the Great Spirit and one committed to the Triune Spirit, the vision quest was a journey into silence and listening. Vision comes as gift, not product. It comes as discerned not deduced. It is an answer to prayer.

Ultimately, the question of whether visions are corporate or individual depends on one's theology. Some people believe God has a plan for their lives. Others believe that God honors whatever directions we choose for our lives and will remain faithful. This is not to say that some choices are not more holy than other ones but only that God's eternal faithfulness to us means that God is with us wherever the journey takes us.

In the end, the warrior returns to his tribe and the Celtic pilgrim returns to her community. We live out our discernment about the future God yearns for us in the context of our communities—whether it's Abram with Sarai, or Lot with the nomadic tribesmen who attached themselves to their family, or Jesus among the twelve, we are all firmly placed in relationships and cannot reach our destination in isolation. A person cannot find wellness without finding wholeness. It is for this reason that family therapists, although willing to do individual consultations with members of the family, insist on treating the whole family as a unit. Similarly, clergy can adopt healthy lifestyles and effective stress-reducing techniques, but unless the congregation they serve is also renewed by a new vision and the power of God, the clergyperson will inevitably find himself or herself simply going through the motions, mired in maintenance instead of motivated for mission.

The renewal of the Church begins with the renewal of the clergy but it cannot be sustained apart from a renewal of both leader and congregation.

"Give us your vision, Lord, this is our prayer.
O, help us to see when the way is not clear,
And gift us with wisdom and lead us, we pray.
Let grace be our calling and our strength for today."
    —New words to the traditional Irish ballad melody *(Slane)*

ℰⅩℴ

Note

1. George Barna, *The Power of Vision* (Ventura, CA: Regal Books, 2003), 24.

Visioning as a Child of God on a Mission

Scott B. Hayashi

The Metra Rail express train to Chicago is always crowded. With the recent turmoil in the economy, the express train has become more crowded. Metra Rail has a list of "considerations" regarding passenger etiquette. These are not always followed. One enforced by the conductors and by the passengers is, "No seats are reserved," in other words, no saving seats for friends. In spite of this policy, there are usually a few people who attempt to save seats. They place their parcels on the bench seat next to them, some try sitting in the middle seat; others scowl as people approach them. The people who try to save seats will usually be seated at the front of the car where the bench seats face each other. These seats are always the last to fill because people would rather look at the back of another person's head than accidentally make eye contact with someone seated across from them.

There is a woman who rides the eight o'clock express who always tries to save two seats for her friends. This woman is well known to the other passengers. She employs the scowl and the "parcels" tactics to ward off fellow riders from seating themselves in her area. On a recent commute to Chicago, there were absolutely no seats remaining in the car other than the two seats she was guarding. She gave me the warning look as I eyed the seat facing her. When I moved to the seat anyway she glared at me, made an angry grunt, and snatched up her bags. Now that the barrier was broken, within a second, another rider plopped himself next to her. We rode in uneasy silence towards Chicago. Every few minutes she would grunt angrily, fidget in her seat, glare at me then stare out the window. The two other passengers, the fellow seated next to me, and the fellow seated next to her busied themselves with their cell phones. Inwardly, I was gleeful and gloating. How dare she try to save seats? Who does she think she is? I showed her didn't I? Glare at me will you? It was a good thing I was not wearing a button that says, "Ask me about the Episcopal Church!"

The emotional and spiritual atmosphere remained tense as we made our way to Chicago's Union Station. My initial glee faded as I began to think about the woman across from me. Perhaps she has a miserable job.

79

Perhaps her marriage is failing. Perhaps one of the few joys she has is sitting with a couple of friends as she rides to work. Regardless of what her story might be, one thing was true: there was more to this woman than just the unhappy person across from me. While I was justified sitting across from her, my satisfaction with her angry disappointment was neither compassionate nor an expression of any of the values that I hold to be at my core. In that moment, I was acutely aware I was not fulfilling my vision of who I am or what I believe I am called to be in this life. I resolved to try to do something to make the situation better.

The tense atmosphere remained as we drew closer to Chicago. I thought about ways that I might ease the tension when the conductor came on the intercom with the usual reminder to not leave our tickets, baggage, briefcases, and other items on the train. On this morning, however, the conductor decided to add some levity into his announcement by asking the passengers to search carefully around to *really* make certain that we were not forgetting something, and then he added a long list of additional items that we might possibly have brought on board. He spoke in a rapid, staccato monotone. It seemed as if he would never stop. As the announcement continued, the passengers began to look at one another in wonder. When he concluded the passengers remained silent, waiting to see if he would start up again.

Across from me the woman was still glum. The fellow next to me was still fiddling with his cell phone. I turned to him and said, "You got that?"

He gave a slight smile and said, "I don't think so." The man across from him looked at the two of us and gave a rueful smile and said, "Yeah, I think I'm going to leave my children on the train." Across from me, the woman's mouth curved into a slight smile. The two men stood to make their way off the train. I looked at the woman across from me. I smiled at her and said, "Why don't you go first." She smiled at me and said, "No, you go on." I looked her in the eye and said, "You have a really good day, alright?" She gave me another smile and thanked me. In those last few moments, the emotional and spiritual field of that little part of the world was made better.

The vision that God has for this world is simple. The world is to be the place where people love one another as Christ loves us. The world is to be the place where God reigns in the hearts, minds, and souls of all people. The Christian's role in this vision is to help "restore all people to unity with God and each other in Christ." (Book of Common Prayer, 855)

For a Christian, any discussion about visioning in life must take as its starting place God's vision for this world. The question should not be, how do I fit God into my vision of my life? The question should be, does my vision of my life help to bring about God's vision of this world? Christ is the vine. We are the branches. Apart from Christ, as Jesus says in the Gospel According to St. John, we can do nothing. (John 15:4-5)

The practice of visioning for a Christian is always a missionary endeavor; God's vision of the world guides/informs the individual Christian's vision as a healer/restorer for the world that God has made. Visioning for the Christian is discerning the ways that he or she might most fully be the embodiment of God's vision for the world. It does not matter if the "world" one participates in is international, local, familial, or even four seats on a train.

The Christian is an active participant in the process. He or she does not simply sit and wait for God to make all things clear. Clarity comes in small pieces as the Christian lives out his or her vision in the world.

If the Christian person is called to be the embodiment of God's vision for the world, then the process of visioning must be carried out with honesty, courage, and prayerful reflection. The Christian brings his or her whole self to the visioning process, including the data or information one accumulates throughout life.

In this process it is helpful to have some guiding questions upon which to reflect:

1. Where are you now?
2. Where are you going?
3. Where do you want to be?
4. How are you going to get there?

Where are you now?

Where are you in regard to:

1. Your relationships
2. Your health—spiritual, emotional, and physical
3. Your finances
4. Your vocation

Reflect prayerfully upon your life and make an honest assessment of exactly where you are. Because people are frequently overly self-critical and, at times, in denial, asking people you trust to help you with these questions may be fruitful.

Is God's vision of restoration and healing present in these areas of your life?

Where are you going?

If you continue with your life as it is right now, making no changes, where do you see yourself going? Imagine yourself five, ten, or fifteen years in the future. What do your relationships, your health, your finances, and your career look like? Do you like what you see?

Brian (not his real name), a friend, told me that he looked at his family life and realized that if he did not change the way he was behaving he would lose his marriage. Brian had friends he trusted. He was confident that even if he did not change course that his friends would still be supportive. But he also believed that if he and his wife divorced there would be ripples throughout the lives of his friends and neighbors. He did not think that he was responsible for their lives or that he "owed" them anything. It just seemed to him that it would subtly change, in a negative way, the spiritual and emotional field of which he was a part. It was nothing that he could define concretely or specifically, "It was just a feeling," he said.

Brian and his wife had not separated, but they had grown apart and their relationship, while not hostile, was, as he described it, tired and confining. He looked into the future and imagined selling his home, seeing his children only on weekends, and feeling responsible for destroying his children's sense of security in the world. He imagined himself as a single man who would have the freedom to be alone at the grocery store at 10:30 at night flipping through a magazine. "Some freedom, huh?" he said.

Where do you want to be?

Perhaps in answering this question you find you are completely satisfied with where you see yourself in the future. If not, then where do you want to be? Imagine yourself in that place. What do you look like? Do you stand straighter? Do you smile more? How do the people with whom you are in relationship seem? Your family, co-workers, friends? What are you able to do that you are not able to do now?

Brian looked forward and did not like the picture of the future that he imagined if he stayed on his current path. He believed that God had blessed him when his wife had given birth to their two children. He wanted to restore a healthy relationship with his wife. He wanted to be an agent of healing for his children, whom he felt had suffered because of the "marriage in name only" that his relationship with his wife had become.

He imagined himself more fully engaged with his wife. He saw them going out to dinner together, just the two of them. He saw himself as more energetic and relaxed, able to care for himself and his family in a deeper way. He imagined that he would be more willing to reach out to others in need. He liked this vision of himself and believed that it represented who he truly was, the one that God had created him to be.

How are you going to get there?

If, as a Christian you are the embodiment of God's vision for the world, then it is not enough to only imagine what life would be like if you made the changes that would bring you to where you want to be. You must fulfill the vision. As Mahatma Gandhi said, "Be the change you want to see in the world."

What steps need to be taken to fulfill/be the vision? What can be done immediately? Who can help? Who will you tell? What can you afford, in terms of finances and time? Do you need to sacrifice something?

One of the sacrifices that Brian made was his self-image of being self-sufficient. He prided himself on being able to figure things out for himself. In this instance, he confessed that he did not know what to do. Everything that he tried was a variation of something he had already tried. He reached the point at which he realized that if he did not know what to do, then how could he do it? Prayer did not bring any answers. He had hoped that God would tell him what to do. God's silence did convince him of one thing, he needed to speak with another human being. It was at that point that he asked me if I knew a good counselor.

To become this vision of himself, he took the first step in admitting that he did not know what to do. The second step was to speak to someone about his situation. The third step was to make a phone call to the person

I recommended. For this step, he asked me to help him by checking with him within a week to make certain that he made the call.

Brian slowly changed and his marriage did improve. He came to understand that somewhere in his life he had lost touch with himself. His efforts to change were guided by the vision of himself as he believed God intended him to be. He wanted to be that person. He desired this not just for himself; he wanted to be this person for his family, his friends, and for the world.

Visioning, as I have presented it, is not a practice to discern whether or not a person should choose between job A or job B, to buy or rent a home, or to make any other choices, large or small. The process that I have presented may help in those decisions and I do it recommend it to anyone who is seeking clarity regarding a choice that they need to make. For me, visioning is the practice of helping a person to live life as a child of God, one who is on a mission to make God's vision of this world a reality. As I said above, it does not matter if the world in which one participates is international, or local and familial, as it was for Brian. Or, as it was for me on one morning in Illinois, a world comprised of four seats on a train.

PRACTICE

How Do I Respond to God's Calling?

It is hard to let go of the past, and yet, until we do, there is no hope whatsoever that we ever gain from the future.

—Benedict of Nursia

The third stage in the identity cycle will be to address the question, What Practical Steps Should I Take? or framed in a different way, How Do I Respond To God's Calling? This is a vocational perspective, thinking through an array of options and moving forward with measurable and growth-oriented steps along our Christian pilgrimage.

The Rev. Sam Portaro candidly shares his personal experience in his essay, "Practicing a Life of Prayer." He offers two simple yet subtly challenging spiritual practices to enrich our prayer lives and lead us into a rich sense of wellness and relationships.

Approaching happiness as a broad, complex field of feelings, Dr. Joe Stewart-Sicking suggests that there are many paths, and offers a set of daily practices that may lead to emotional well-being and as his essay subtitle suggests, "Finding Joy that Is Complete."

Dr. Elaine Hollensbe introduces the complexity and challenges of emotional work. Often in our daily life, we are expected to express situationally appropriate emotions and, in some cases, suppress emotions we actually feel. She points out the positive and negative consequences of emotional labor and offers strategies to manage emotions that can guide us to wellness.

As a physician and priest, the Rev. Dr. Bill Watson suggests that care of our mind, body, and spirit will not only enrich the quality of our lives, but also will bring us into a closer relationship with our neighbors and with God. His emphasis on the importance of exercise, such as simply walking, can positively affect our physical health as well as our mind, spirit, and our awareness of God's presence in our lives.

As a university professor and a multi-tasking father of four children, Dr. Glen Kreiner writes from practical experience and academic authority about managing boundaries between work and home. Recognizing the challenges in today's demanding and frenetic life, he shares practical tactics to address and balance work-home boundary issues.

In her conversational style of writing, Phyllis Strupp, a financial planner, suggests ways to think about the power of money in our lives, and challenges us with the concept that we can become stewards rather than owners of worldly wealth.

Practicing a Life of Prayer

Sam Portaro

"I used to have a prayer life."

That's a fairly common sentiment, sometimes spoken, but more often carried silently in the recesses of our hearts, arising in those harried moments when we feel far, far away from the riches of relationship with God. And therein lies a key to understanding the variable nature of spiritual life and practice: it's about relationship.

We speak often, and, I think, far too glibly, of relationship with God. Relationship with a living God, like any committed relationship between two people, is organic. It begins with fervor, enthusiasm, not a little infatuation, and all the practices we associate with the first blush of love. We dote and are doted upon, sometimes to the point of obsession. We're eager to please, and quick to search out all the little things that might endear us to the other. In the human realm this entails long letters or email posts, extravagant gifts, huge telephone bills, and that dumbstruck expression of total distraction. In the spiritual realm it can mean frequent attendance at worship, retreats, a fascination with ritual, incessant reading in the mystics and early church saints, exploration of rosaries, labyrinths, centering prayer and the Ignatian exercises—all those practices you might expect to read about in essays like this one (but won't).

In the dating phase of human romance, we're keen to put on our best face, show off our knowledge of good food, wine, the most interesting entertainments and, of course, our scintillating wit. But as the relationship grows and matures, formality gives way to greater ease, casualness, regularity. Things change, as they should. In the matter of human relationships, we have come to accept such alterations as normal. After all, none of us can sustain the obsessions of early courtship for long. Besides, we'd never get anything else done.

So why do we find it surprising that a relationship with God might be any different? Perhaps because we've never really been taught or encouraged otherwise. Yet the evidence is abundant.

Take Moses, for example. When, as an adult, he first encounters God, it's at that famous burning bush. The encounter comes unbidden, a surprise initiated by God. It's so disorienting Moses has to be guided through this rare moment in the presence of this amazing love that has sought and found him. Moses is thunderstruck, so smitten he does not demur when God demands he do a very intimate thing, at least for people of his time and culture: Moses takes off his shoes. There's a lot in that symbol, as in so many actions between people in the early moments of what may ultimately prove to be the relationship of a lifetime. Baring his feet, Moses signifies his respect and enters the intimacy of the moment. Removing one's sandals was one of the first acts upon entering another's tent or house, a sign of receptive vulnerability, that one accepts the hospitality offered, that one is there to stay a while.

But as Moses and God progress beyond that initial meeting, their relationship changes. Years later, while toiling thanklessly to encourage the people of Israel to abandon the familiar comforts of slavery in Egypt and enter into relationship with this wildly unknown God, Moses reaches the kind of exasperation any experienced partner will readily recognize. The unseen God has been big on encouragement but a little absent in the hands-on department and Moses has reached the end of his short tether. Uprooted and with no destination on the horizon, the people are tired, and Moses is most certainly weary of wandering the wilderness without benefit of Google Maps or GPS, much less fast food outlets. The same Moses who had once been awed by a dazzling desert fire is now ablaze himself. He unleashes a pretty hot earful for God which basically says, "I've had it up to the yin-yang with these griping, ungrateful people you claim to be so fond of. Get up off your holy hind end and pull your weight!" And God does.

So to anyone who says aloud or in the depths of the despairing heart, I used to have a prayer life, I suggest that you probably still do have a prayer life. It's just different now. As it should be. Because you are different, and God is different from that time you first locked metaphorical eyes and set off on this wonderful life together. One would hope that you've matured. Both of you. Yes, God matures. Read the Hebrew Scriptures. It's all there. God is a living God. God gets disappointed, and angry. A lot of water flows under Noah's ark and over Mount Ararat, but God does grow. And that's only one example.

The apostle Paul understood maturation in faith. He speaks of it often in his letters to the early believers. Some are essentially infants. Some have progressed to more solid food. And, presumably, some actually make it to adulthood. If your prayer life has changed, it's quite likely that you are no longer where you used to be.

Now it's true that this could mean that you have drifted away from God. That does happen, even as space sometimes expands between me and my partner when I grow preoccupied with my projects, or find myself away from home for weeks on end, or begin to take our relationship for granted, or all of the above. When this happens, a little self-discipline may be called for. I'll adjust or change my calendar, pay more attention to our life together, actually make a real date—a space and time devoted to enriching and renewing our relationship with one another. Sometimes we have to do the same thing in our relationship with God. go away on retreat, set aside time for prayer or worship, or whatever it is that brings us back into a centered relationship with our divine partner.

But you and God are never so far apart as it seems. Certainly, God hasn't gone anywhere. Likely it's just that you relate to one another differently now. At the very least, it's not all about you two anymore. That may be how it started out, just me and God. In those early dating days, in those first passionate embraces, we were caught up in the rarified realm of infatuation and romantic preoccupation. But the honeymoon's over. There's a mortgage, and maybe kids, and the laundry's piling up. Or to use another set of familiar images, there's a vestry, and maybe a youth group, and the list of shut-ins and hospital visitations is multiplying.

But you're still in the relationship. And you still have a prayer life, a rich spiritual repository. It's just different now. My partner and I have been together over thirteen years. Chris is a second-grade teacher, so we treasure our summers as a special time to be together. But this summer's been a bear. His mother's terminal cancer ramped up in May and took her life in June, so Chris was back and forth from Illinois to Oregon tending to his family, and more weeks were devoured by funeral preparations and family obligations. Then a large contingent of my family came to visit, filling every bed in our house for another week. No sooner had we washed all the linens than a longtime friend suffered the death of a family member in Chicago, calling upon our hospitality and filling all our beds for another week. Now we're hosting a European cousin, his wife, and their new baby daughter. Yet in every act of hospitality and grace extended to each other's families and friends, in every load of laundry and every meal prepared, every sorrow listened to and every joke relished, we've expressed our love for one another. As Jesus admonished, whenever we act with grace, generosity, and kindness to others, we're expressing love for God.

In my relationship with God I have rarely prayed in the traditional oracular sense. God knows (literally) the secrets of my heart; we long ago came to an understanding on that. But in every moment spent pondering the scriptures, sitting in thought and crafting sentences, God and I are in conversation. When I read, when I study the scriptures, I engage a conversation that allows the other to speak to me. When I write, I engage a conversation that includes those to whom I have listened, those who have spoken to me, and those to whom I speak or write.

When we distinguish too sharply between our daily activity and our prayer we indulge an unhealthy compartmentalization that diminishes both. Just as in human relationship we learn to express our very real love in small, even mundane gestures throughout our daily interactions, so in our relationship with God we may come to see, show, and speak the love between us in the ordinary. When we see the whole of our lives as an incarnate medium of prayer, we find integrity—wholeness—and fullness of life. We pray with the whole of ourselves, in the giving of our all to God, just as we promised in our baptism.

Indeed, integrity is the mark of life's fullness, the abundance promised in John 10:10, where Jesus claims to have come that we might have life in all its fullness. An integrated life saturated by the prayer of human action is a rich spirituality. And it is transformative. To see our daily activities not as tasks to be ticked off a to-do list but as opportunities and expressions of prayer, occasions to share communion with God, is to change—to re-value, literally to re-deem—every occasion. Activities are no longer valued for having been completed, but are treasured for what has been shared. A meeting becomes more than an agenda to get through; it becomes an opportunity to share with others in the stewardship of responsibility. A conversation with another person in counsel or direction or just in passing is an invitation into discourse with God, who may speak to us in what the other has to say, or in what we hear ourselves say in response to the question uttered by God's incarnation seated across from us.

I recall vividly and warmly an occasion when a young rector, totally exhausted and overwhelmed by the demands of a growing congregation and a growing family, confessed sadly the poverty of his prayer life. His sense of despair was palpable. I asked him if he'd ever stood by his child's bed, watching that sleeping child in the dim light, and felt the profound awareness of the beautiful mystery there before him. As though I had seen into the recesses of his most private thoughts, he nodded in affirmation. Then,

I suggested to him, "You have stood on holy ground and in that moment you have known the presence of God. Isn't that what we pray most fervently to know? Are we not like the winsome friends of A.A. Milne's *Winnie the Pooh*, Piglet, when 'sidled up to Pooh from behind?'

"Pooh?" he whispered.

"Yes, Piglet?"

"Nothing," said Piglet, taking Pooh's hand. "I just wanted to be sure of you."[1]

God gives each of us such moments as this young father knew, as Piglet knew in Pooh's hand. Why, then, deny ourselves the experience of this gift of our deepest prayer answered?

Apparently, no one had ever made such a connection for the young rector. As his life and ministry had changed and grown, as responsibilities had expanded and the stewardship of time and energies shifted, no one had ever suggested that his spirituality, his prayer, might also take on new shapes, demand new practices. No one had ever thought to draw the line that connected this young father at his child's bedside to Moses, or to the long journey of the magi who searched for ultimate wisdom and the fullness of divine power and found all that and more swaddled in a cradle.

Having written at length of the full integration of spirituality into our lives, I offer only two spiritual practices, each embodied in phrases common to our everyday experiences. They are homely, ordinary, and spontaneous. But don't be fooled. These are two profoundly difficult disciplines to maintain, especially in our times and in our culture.

The first spiritual practice is this: pay attention.

This is genuine sacrifice, to pay something of real value. My attention is exceedingly valuable. Commercial interests are paying huge sums of money for it; billions are spent every day for ads vying for my attention. The phone rings, the email beckons. I'm bombarded. Lord knows I try to hold it all at bay. Still, I confess that I lose a little ground every day. I have to be more intentional about paying attention, about being a steward of the gift of attention God has given me.

A good beginning is just to embrace the value of attention. The happy outcome of the culture's commodification of attention is that by assigning a dollar value to a minute of my TV-viewing or radio-listening time, measuring my attention to the web site, the newspaper, or the magazine in terms of money, I am more aware of how my attention constitutes a currency. My attention, which is made of my time, consideration, and talent directed toward someone or something else, is limited. I have only a finite

amount on deposit. Like writing a check or picking a stock, I want to be
more judicious in how, where, and why I spend it. Annie Dillard wisely
counseled, "Spend the afternoon. You can't take it with you."[2] We are
spending not just the afternoon, but our entire lives. Time is the currency
of God's economy.

Moreover, paying attention is part of my giving to God, to neighbor,
and to self. Am I paying attention to the people and concerns that have
greatest value for me, that represent love for God, neighbor, and self? Am
I giving the first fruits of my attention, the best of my attention to God?
Or am I squandering it, throwing my precious attention away, tossing it
down the proverbial rat hole, flushing it down the great cosmic toilet?

Pay attention. Pay it thoughtfully. Give your attention as you would
your most precious gift, for indeed, it's worth as much and more. It's your
life, the life God has given you, the only life you have in this world. Pay
attention gratefully, out of love for the gift of attention itself, the marvel-
ous gift of awareness that raises our stature above even the angels.

Pay attention to the present moment, to the child standing at your
knee pulling on your pant leg. Pay it to the person sitting across the room
hardly aware of your presence, that other child of God over there caught
up in his own world, overwhelmed by her own distractions. Pay it to the
clerk at the grocery checkout who hasn't smiled all day, hasn't smiled in
so long because she's so seldom seen a smile across the scanner.

Paying attention is not easy, not in a day filled with myriad distractions and demands and a culture that in so many ways encourages a
self-centered sense of entitlement. Just as I must in some instances be
especially careful of where I put my feet, lest I fall, stumble, or slip, so I
have occasionally to remind myself to pause, to be mindful of where I put
my attention, my heart. While a conscious effort may be required at the
outset, like any practice followed regularly, the pause becomes familiar.
So does the reward. When I pay attention, I don't have to remind myself
of God's presence in my life; God is nearly always present and manifest,
recognizable in the other, the one in whom and to whom I have paid my
attention. Pay attention.

The second spiritual practice is this: take care.

It rolls off the tongue easily, usually as we part. Take care, we say. The
inference, of course, is be careful, a reminder to be more mindful. Take
care of yourself, and of others.

But I emphasize the verb "take." *Take* care. Receive, reach out, and seize
hold of care. That's counterintuitive for us Christians; our vocabulary is

mostly about giving, sacrificing, doing unto. Taking feels somehow heretical. We're discouraged from seeking, wanting, or taking anything for ourselves.

And *that's* the heresy. The gospel is all about good news for us, about what God has done, is doing, for me and for you. It's about the gift of life freely offered to each of us. In a backward, upside down way, we've come to believe ourselves totally unworthy, undeserving of any gift. No matter that the unworthiness and undeserving were intended to impress upon us that what God gives us is a gift, not something we earn. What was said is not what we heard; what we heard was that it is only blessed to give, that there is no blessing ever in receiving.

Taking care is hard for us. We're fiercely independent, and proud of it. We hate any suggestion that we need anything, cringe beneath any and every concern directed our way. It makes us seem weak, needy, un-American, so we resist care.

But *take* the care that God holds out, offers in the hands of those who reach out to help. Take the care proffered in those friends God gives us, who manifest God's love in the flesh, the companions who are there for us, and with us in the inevitable dark nights, those who believe in us, love us even when we find it hard to believe in or love ourselves. *Take* the care that comes running to the door and leaps into your arms, happy that you're home, whether it's the love of your child, or the love of your dog. Take the care that comes your way, receive it as the gift of God that it is, and know that the blessedness of giving extends in equal measure to the blessedness of receiving.

Making these connections, discerning the ways that God continues to court us, to nurture us, to touch and hold us in all the mundane matters of our lives may be the most important spiritual discipline of the mature believer. Not learning a new or better way to pray, not seeking ever more archaic or clever or elegant or technologically sophisticated ways to speak to God, but discerning—which is a form of listening with eyes, ears, heart, and soul to the God who seeks to express the most profound love we can ever know. It's not something we find easy, or do well. I know.

But I'm getting better. Now the gift comes more frequently. Most often like it came to that young parent standing in the moonlight at the child's bedside. In those odd instances when I'm paying attention to my partner, a colleague, or a stranger, or any of the ways the incarnate God is present to us in the person and the moment. In the briefest of moments, it washes over me, that surprising, mysterious awareness and appreciation of what it means to be in the heart of God, simply but profoundly loved just as we are.

Pay attention. Take care. Two spiritual practices. One invites us to give, the other to receive; each presents a challenge, and demands the sacrifice of something dear to us. But the gift is great; where once we used to have a prayer life, we find we have a life of prayer.

∞

Notes

1. A. A. Milne, *Winnie-the-Pooh*.
2. Annie Dillard, *Pilgrim at Tinker Creek* (New York: Harper, 1974), 269.

Emotional Well-Being:
Finding Joy that Is Complete

J. A. Stewart-Sicking

When I was growing up, I was fascinated by my mother's bookshelf. Though she was then devoted to raising my siblings and me, she was a recovering classics and theology major, and her books were decidedly different from any others my friends' moms had sitting around. There were Latin grammars and Platonic dialogues and books on topics like "nihilism" and the "death of God." They were fascinating and to be honest, when I went to seminary, I cajoled her into giving several of them to my own library. When I was a child, I didn't appreciate how all the books fit together, and frankly, my fascination was more that they were such long books on seemingly straightforward subjects. One in particular stood out, a hefty tome with a title along the lines of *Happiness Here and Hereafter*. I think it was probably a handbook of the ethics of Thomas Aquinas, but as a child, all I could think was that it was really long. Really? You need a five-pound book to tell you about happiness? Doesn't everyone want to be happy? It doesn't seem that difficult to understand—these people need to get outside and play more.

But as I have spent more time studying happiness, it is beginning to seem that a five-pound book on the subject has got to be the abridged version. For something universally sought after and seemingly commonsense, happiness is an unusually difficult idea to comprehend. It seems wise to conclude with prominent psychologists that happiness is a field of study, not a single phenomenon.[1] It is not something that any single perspective can capture. I suppose that this is good news—if happiness were simple, it would hardly be ultimately satisfying. But this complexity makes any discussion of happiness only an invitation into the process of discovery, one that will last until we see God face to face.

Developing a Psychology of Well-Being

Given the amount of attention that theologians and philosophers, such as those represented on my mother's bookshelf, have given to the nature of happiness, it is odd that modern psychology has considered this topic so late in its history. In fact, serious psychological study of happiness has entered the mainstream only in the past decade.

One reason for this neglect may be due to psychology's links to clinical practice. Since the time of Freud, psychologists and related professionals have spent much of their time observing the ways in which people's minds and emotions can break down. Thus, the focus of research and training tended to be on treating pathology and restoring people to "normal" functioning. But over time, scholars and practitioners realized that treatment wasn't enough.[2]

Thus, beginning in the 1960s, many mental health fields began to adopt a more proactive, preventive stance toward emotional problems. But a more radical change began to emerge at the turn of the millennium, with an article by two prominent psychologists suggesting that social science should move beyond its focus on problems (whether treating or preventing them) to one of "flourishing"[3]—a revolutionary term to hear modern social scientists use. The authors suggested that social science can be an important tool for showing people how to live a good life, experience well-being, and thrive in communities. The movement represented by this article, known as "positive psychology," aims to be the "science of happiness," and it has directed attention to the nature of emotional well-being and the paths to attain it.

Hedonic Psychology

One key stream of research for understanding positive psychology comes out of studies on the interplay between positive and negative emotions. Researchers have noticed that positive emotions (such as joy, attentiveness, confidence, and contentment) are relatively independent of negative emotions (such as fear, sadness, and anger)—that is, positive and negative emotions are triggered by different situations, and things that increase the one (like having friends) do not necessarily decrease the other.[4] Clergy provide an important example of this phenomenon: many clergy report that their work is simultaneously engaging and exhausting.[5] Thus, researchers began to realize that positive and negative feelings[6] might not be opposites, but two distinct phenomena. From this perspective, happiness is having a balance of positive and negative feelings, and achieving happiness requires efforts both to boost positive emotions and decrease negative ones.

With this knowledge, an entire approach has developed towards emotional well-being, known as the *hedonic* approach[7] due to its focus on maximizing pleasure and minimizing pain. The hedonic approach defines emotional well-being as subjective well-being, the experience of relatively high levels of positive emotions and low levels of negative emotions, along with a sense that one's entire life has been well-lived and satisfying. From this perspective, the good life is one spent finding ways to maximize the experience of pleasure and minimize the experience of pain.

Eudaimonic Psychology

As straightforward as this formulation is, many psychologists don't find it satisfying. In their view it doesn't seem to capture all there is to being human. And so some psychologists have turned to ancient philosophy to generate a fuller picture of happiness. From Aristotle, they borrowed the concept of *eudaimonia* to describe the life well-lived.[8] This term is sometimes translated as "happiness," but a better translation might be "human flourishing," able to participate in all the aspects of human life that are truly good. And certainly, this concept goes beyond simple considerations of pleasure and pain to include a focus on thriving and achieving one's potential.

Eudaimonic psychologists noted that without a clear theoretical rationale, hedonic psychology had neglected important aspects of psychological well-being,[9] including relationships with one's self and with others. Thus, the eudaimonic approach used philosophy and developmental psychology to define six aspects of psychological well-being:[10] self-acceptance, positive relations with others that show the ability to love and care, a sense of autonomy, a sense of environmental mastery, a sense of purpose in life, and the experience of personal growth.

These six dimensions suggest ways to do a "happiness audit" to understand our own location on the path to flourishing. Just as we might do a holistic assessment of our physical fitness, we can turn to each of these dimensions to gauge our emotional well-being.[11]

To what extent do we own and accept both the good and bad parts of ourselves? To what extent do we have satisfying and caring relationships with others?

To what extent do we honor our own standards of right and wrong? How well do we manage the complexity of our daily affairs?

To what extent do we have goals and beliefs that shape the direction of our lives? And to what degree are we continually growing and improving?

The answers to these questions can give us a better picture of our emotional well-being and possible areas in which to focus our efforts for improvement.

Combining the eudaimonic and hedonic approaches in research has yielded some intriguing results.[12] While some aspects of psychological well-being are strongly related to subjective well-being, there appears to be a real distinction between a pleasurable life and a meaningful life. For many people, psychological well-being and subjective well-being complement one another, with joyfulness and self-acceptance reinforcing one another, or sadness and lack of purpose, forming a vicious cycle. This is what we might expect. But it is possible for people to compensate for the lack of one type of well-being with the presence of another. For instance, people who are more open to new experiences have shown high levels of psychological well-being, but not subjective well-being—they valued themselves and saw their lives as meaningful, yet still were annoyed, sad, or fearful. And many people fall into one of these mixed categories. Moreover, other studies have found that eudaimonia can trump pleasure in predicting life satisfaction, with one researcher noting that "he who dies with the most toys may or may not win, but he will not do so as happily as one who dies after a life of helping others."[13] It seems that a life of caring for self and others is intrinsically worthwhile, something that people of faith have long argued.

Combining the perspectives of hedonic and eudaimonic psychology, we can see that there are many ways to understand happiness, and many routes to achieving emotional well-being. But what helps people get there?

Paths to Happiness

One useful way to think about the factors that affect people's happiness is to break it down into components:

Happiness = personality set-point (50%) + life circumstances (10%)
+ volitional activity (40%).[14]

This equation follows common sense: some level of happiness is built into people's personalities, but life circumstances and personal choices can also impact it. And since personality is not easily changed, it makes sense to focus energy on creating circumstances conducive to happiness and in helping people make the most of their situations—but the real challenge is how to distinguish among the three.

Who is happy?

The good news is that repeatedly, research in the hedonic tradition has shown that most people are happy.[15] But it has also identified a large number of characteristics associated with higher subjective well-being.[16] For instance, demographic factors such as age, gender, class, and ethnicity tend to have weak associations with happiness. The number of friends, religiousness, leisure activity, being married, and personality features show more moderate associations. The strongest associations with subjective well-being are with gratitude, optimism, employment, frequency of sexual intercourse, and self-esteem.

These findings do not make it clear whether happiness causes these characteristics or the characteristics lead to happiness (e.g., Are happy people more likely to marry, or does marriage make people more likely to be happy?), but it is interesting to note a promising pattern: While many of the smaller effects are in personality and life circumstances beyond one's control, many of the large predictors of happiness are actually things that people can change, such as gratitude or optimism. With this in mind, researchers have focused on the potential for people to increase their own happiness.

Daily Best Practices

Increasingly, studies of emotional well-being and happiness are recommending that people consider "daily life best practices to optimize functioning and avert significant problems."[17] The practices they recommend are based on the relationships discussed above and the logic that the best way to impact people's happiness is through focusing on volitional activity.

One promising set of daily practices focuses on developing optimism. Psychologists have long known that people selectively pay attention to the negative—the bad things that happen to us result in more motivation to do something than equally strong positive events.[18] Thus, there is a built-in negativity bias that all human beings have, and a potential benefit for increasing everyone's optimism. The good news is that people can learn optimism through challenging their illogical beliefs that they are responsible for bad things happening, that they are generally set up to have bad things happen to them, and that there is nothing they can change about the situation.[19]

While these exercises were designed to help people with especially pessimistic and self-defeating beliefs, they can also be used to prevent these beliefs from taking hold in the first place. All it takes is attention to thinking patterns or "self-talk." For instance, when we find ourselves engaging in pessimistic thinking, we can ask ourselves questions such as:

1. What is the evidence? What evidence supports this idea? What is the evidence against this idea?

2. Is there an alternative explanation?

3. What's the worst that could happen? Could I live through it? What is the best that could happen? What is the most realistic outcome?

4. What is the effect of my believing this automatic thought? What could be the effect of changing my thinking?

5. What should I do about it?

6. What would I tell _____ (a friend) if he or she were in the same situation?[20]

These questions, originally developed for the treatment of depression, are a useful antidote to pessimistic thoughts even in relatively healthy people.

Another set of exercises for promoting emotional well-being revolve around the practice of gratitude. One common feature of negative emotions is that they lead people to think again and again about what is wrong. The practice of being thankful is a very powerful way to short-circuit this cycle—it re-directs cycles of thinking toward positive things and even one's moral obligations, highlighting ways to find benefits amidst adversity.[21] It is hard think about how much you hate your boss when you are thinking about how grateful you are that you got to take your son to the zoo. And in focusing more and more on the positive aspects of life, gratitude seeks to reverse the built-in negative perception bias without being naïve or self-deceptive. But gratitude takes practice—in identifying non-grateful thoughts, replacing them with grateful thoughts, and translating the feeling of gratitude into action.[22]

Happiness-promoting Environments

While these individual exercises may be helpful in boosting emotional well-being, it is only part of the equation. From a systems perspective, it is also important to foster environments that support happiness.

While there is a great deal of research on the relationship between environmental factors and well-being, for many people, the most important system affecting well-being is the workplace. Not only is employment status strongly associated with emotional well-being, but certain characteristics of the workplace can also have important effects on individual well-being. Healthy workplaces are those in which employees have some autonomy, interpersonal contact, opportunities to use their skills, a variety of tasks, clear and reasonable goals, physical safety, supportive supervision, and adequate rewards for their work.[23] In fact, in CREDO's research with clergy, the most important predictors of vocational satisfaction and well-being were (1) perceived safety to make a mistake, (2) meaningfulness, and (3) the ability to use all of one's gifts Findings such as these, which focus not only on individual experience, but also on how to promote caring and happy systems, suggest that leaders can draw from a much deeper toolbox when working to foster happiness. And these findings from the workplace can be taken directly into congregational leadership. For instance, it may do more to foster the emotional well-being of clergy and lay leaders to encourage a congregational culture that values humor in the face of mistakes than to focus on any particular problem relationships. And ministries might have more vigor if they are framed in the spiritual meaning of discerning and sharing our gifts. Moreover, this systems focus explicitly encourages leaders to focus on issues of justice and community, issues which can be ignored when focusing solely on individual efforts to promote wellness.

Happiness and Abundant Life

Many psychologists would end this discussion with the practices we just discussed. But again, we must ask, "Is that all there is?" No discussion of happiness can be complete if it doesn't consider spiritual and theological points of view. In fact, in psychology there is a remarkable momentum to current discussions of happiness: scholars are beginning to quote Aristotle on ethics and recommend daily exercises to achieve true happiness. In many ways, modern positive psychology is reviving the practice of ancient philosophy that devoted itself to practicing a way of life that could produce true happiness.[24] Christian spirituality came out of this very same soil, adapting ancient philosophy to open human beings toward the divine.[25] Thus, positive psychology's momentum towards developing happiness through practices seems like a perfect example of the theological principle that the natural human quest for happiness will inevitably need an answer in the supernatural wisdom of God's revelation in Christ.[26]

The Vision of God

Given the strong affinity between positive psychology and ancient ethics, especially in the work of Aristotle, it is instructive to look at how the greatest Christian student of Aristotle relates the human quest for happiness to the spiritual quest for beatitude. In book II–I of his *Summa Theologica*, Thomas Aquinas takes on the issue of happiness directly.[27]

First, he considers whether or not happiness exists in pleasure (which we might call the hedonic psychology hypothesis). He notes that delight is not happiness itself but is accidental to it—a result of resting in the fullness of the Good—and thus it will always accompany true happiness, but is not the same thing. In fact, in this life, delight can become a distraction from the true pursuit of happiness, because we can become stuck enjoying a lesser good—whether it be chocolate, success, or "spiritual" experiences—instead of moving on to something greater.

So what is true happiness? Aquinas suggests that happiness exists in the vision of God—it is that perfection, granted to us by grace, where we can rest in knowing and seeing God face to face, mystically united to God. In this state of blessedness, there is nothing more for us to seek, because we have this highest goal for which we were created. But only the good—those infused with the virtue of love—can see God, for to see God is to love God, which is to love the good. So Aquinas links true happiness with goodness, just as in the beatitude: "Blessed are the pure in heart, for they shall see God." (Matthew 5:8) Happiness is invariably ethical. And while Aquinas notes that perfect and true happiness cannot be had in this life, he contends that a certain participation in this true happiness can be attained, and it is attained through engaging the imperfectly good things of this world led by the virtues, especially faith, hope, and love.

If happiness even in this life involves goodness, then consideration of emotional well-being is in some ways inseparable from consideration of spiritual well-being. And lack of attention to the moral and the spiritual is likely to prevent us from achieving true happiness in this life. Joy is a fruit of the spirit, as Paul would remind us (Galatians 5:22) and there are several moral and spiritual concerns that can be thwarted by an exclusive focus on emotional well-being. Balanced emotions do not guarantee an attention to justice. Self-acceptance can easily devolve into self-indulgence. The pursuit of delight outside of the greater pursuit of God can lead to gluttony or lustfulness. And gratitude is ultimately directed to God.

Worshipful Life

But Aquinas's account also notes that paying attention to the spirit without care for the senses and body is just as fruitless. Later in his discussion of happiness, he notes that a body is necessary for full happiness, since human beings were created to be embodied.[28] So in pursuing spiritual well-being, we should not neglect emotional well-being—we are not angels, but embodied souls. And when understood within the broader context of a life oriented to life in the Spirit, psychological understandings of emotional well-being are invaluable aids to honoring the body and mind given to us in creation.

So how does emotional well-being fit in? It is part of a whole, and not separate from the abundant life promised to followers of Jesus. For our joy is made complete when we share in Christ's joy, abiding in the Father's love. (John 15:10-11) Somehow, we won't be truly happy unless we are in love with God and share that love with the world. In turn, the emotional well-being that we cultivate bears witness to the glory of the God we love. As Irenaeus of Lyons summarizes these mysteries: "the glory of God is a [human being] fully alive; and the true life of [human beings] consists in beholding God."[29] Emotional well-being is part of a life best described as complete worship,[30] where the embodied human being's true joy comes through glimpses of God in daily life and in responding to them in gratitude.

So happiness here is inextricably linked with happiness hereafter. Emotional well-being is to be cultivated precisely because it is in service to spiritual ends, and both are necessary for the life abundant. So cultivate daily practices for emotional well-being and think about the ways in which you can pursue the many facets of well-being in your own life and in those of others. And as you do this, become open through these practices to the true source of joy. For then, your joy will be complete.

℘

Notes

1. Martin E. P. Seligman and others. 2005. Positive psychology progress: empirical validation of interventions, *American Psychologist* 60 no. (5) 410–421.

2. Robert K. Conyne, *Preventive Counseling: Helping People to Become Empowered in Systems and Settings (2nd Ed.)* (New York: Brunner-Routledge, 2004) 236.

3. Martin E. P. Seligman and Mihaly Csikszentmihalyi. 2000. Positive psychology: an introduction *American Psychologist* 55: 1, 5–14.

4. David Watson, Positive affectivity: the disposition to experience pleasurable emotional states, C. R. Snyder and Shane J. Lopez, eds. (New York: Oxford University Press, 2002), 106–119. In *Handbook of Positive Psychology*, eds.

5. Leslie J. Francis, P. Kaldor, M. Robbins, and K. Castle. 2005. Happy but exhausted? work-related psychological health among clergy. *Pastoral Science*, 24, 101–120.

6. N. Bradburn, *The Structure of Psychological Well-being* (Chicago: Aldine, 1969).

7. Edward L. Deci and Richard M. Ryan. 2008. "Hedonia, eudaimonia, and well-being: an introduction," 1989. *Journal of Happiness Studies* 9. 1, 1–11.

8. C. Ryff. Happiness is everything, or is it?: explorations on the meaning of psychological well-being, *Journal of Personality and Social Psychology*, 57, 1069–1081.

9. Ibid.

10. Ibid.

11. Extended descriptions of these six dimensions can be found in Carol D. Ryff and Corey L. Keyes. 1995. The structure of psychological well-being revisited. *Journal of Personality and Social Psychology* 69, 719–727.

12. Corey L. M. Keyes, Dov Shmotkin and Carol D. Ryff. 2002. Optimizing well-being: the empirical encounter of two traditions, *Journal of Personality and Social Psychology*, 82, 6, 1007–1022.

13. Ibid., 7.9

14. Sonja Lyubomirsky, Kennon M. Sheldon and David Schkade. 2005. Pursuing happiness: the architecture of sustainable change, *Review of General Psychology*, 9.(2), 111–131. The percentages are based on the amount of variation in happiness that each factor tends to account for in empirical studies.

15. Ed Diener and Carol Diener. 1996. Most people are happy. *Psychological Science* 7, (3), 181–185.

16. *Peterson's Primer in Positive Psychology*, 386, 92 gives a useful table summarizing this research. It is worth noting that these results are derived from the more dominant hedonic approach. Eudaimonic psychology has tended to focus on demographic and social factors and less on those areas in which personal volition comes into play.

17. Conyne, *Preventive Counseling*, 36.

18. Tiffany A. Ito and John T. Cacioppo, The psychophysiology of utility appraisals In *Well-being: The Foundations of Hedonic Psychology*, eds. Daniel Kahneman, Ed Diener and Norbert Schwarz, (New York: Russell Sage Foundation, 1999), 470–488.

19. Aaron T. Beck, *Cognitive Therapy of Depression* (New York: Guilford Press, 1979) calls this set of beliefs the "depressive triad" for its commonality among those struggling with clinical depression.

20. Judith S. Beck, *Cognitive Therapy: Basics and Beyond* (New York: Guilford Press, 1995), 109.

21. Robert A. Emmons and Charles M. Shelton, *Handbook of Positive Psychology*, eds. C. R. Snyder and Shane J. Lopez (New York: Oxford University Press, 2002), 459–471.

22. Ibid.

23. Peter Warr, "Well-being and the Workplace" in *Well-being: The Foundations of Hedonic Psychology*, eds. Daniel Kahneman, Ed Diener and Norbert Schwarz (New York, NY, US: Russell Sage Foundation, 1999), 392–412.

24. Pierre Hadot, *Philosophy as a Way of Life: Spiritual Exercises from Socrates to Foucault* [Exercices spirituels et philosophie antique.], ed. Arnold Ira Davidson, trans. Michael Chase (Malden, MA: Blackwell, 1995).

25. Ibid.

26. This is a guiding principle of Aquinas and much of Roman Catholic, Anglican, and Eastern Orthodox theology. Reformed and Lutheran theologians tend to be suspicious of any claims that human knowledge could know anything that could prepare for or point to the revelation of God in Christ. But one doesn't need to accept secular psychology as *preparatio evangelica* to see that it will inevitably need to engage questions of spirituality and life's ultimate meaning that Christianity has strong claims about from revelation.

27. Thomas Aquinas, *Summa Theologica*, trans. Dominicans of the English Province, 1st complete American ed. (New York: Benziger Bros., 1947).

28. Ibid., II–I.Q4.5.

29. Irenaeus of Lyons, "Against Heresies" in *The Ante-Nicene Fathers. Translations of the Writings of the Fathers Down to A.D. 325*, eds. Alexander Roberts and others (New York: C. Scribner's Sons, 1900), IV.XX.7.

30. Kenneth E. Kirk, *The Vision of God: The Christian Doctrine of the Summum Bonum*, Pbk. ed. (Harrisburg, PA: Morehouse Publishing, 1991).

Wellness Begins With A Walk

William J. Watson, III

Monday is the most stressful day in many professional offices, particularly in a family practice office. A weekend's worth of problems must be addressed in addition to the regularly scheduled appointments. When I finally finish seeing all the patients and responding to all the calls it is often quite late. By the time I arrive home, I am emotionally spent. After many years of trial and error, I discovered that if I went for a walk after supper, the stress of the day seemed to melt away. The result of walking was almost paradoxical. Rather than being tired, I was calm and alert and much more present to my family. Walking thus became a very important way for me to care for myself.

The call to care for mind, body, and spirit is rooted in God's desire for us. God desires our love. The dimensions of that love are framed in the great commandment. We are to love God with all our heart, soul, strength, and mind. (Luke 10:27) God's love involves all of who we are, all aspects of our lives. This love is intimately a part of us enfleshed, as God's love for us in the incarnation. We are responding to the love that formed us and has known us from the womb.

To live into the great commandment requires every aspect of our being. Yet, as a society we have become, to a certain extent, lost in our heads. Many of us spend inordinate amounts of time in worlds that exist solely within our imaginations. We walk about in reveries of our own creation. Ear buds have become our most common fashion accessory. We walk about in proximity but signaling our desire to be left alone. We want to be left in our heads. Our lives exist only in our minds.

Technology increasingly promises us fulfillment in worlds of our own creation. We interact in cyberspace in ways that require little of our bodies except the ability to handle a mouse or tap a few keys. We spend more and more time interacting with technology rather than each other. We devote ourselves to surfing the Internet, playing video games, or responding to email, blogs, or MySpace and Facebook pages. We may even go so far as to create avatars, imaginary lives projected into cyberspace. Living in another dimension in space, we may feel that don't need our bodies. With such technological advancement, why should we care for the body? We may begin to see our bodies as existing simply to support our head and hands. But the great commandment calls us out of our heads and into our bodies.

Response to that commandment requires us to become reacquainted with our bodies. Jean Denton wrote, "A spirituality of health cannot remain in the realm of the head, but must work itself into our fingers and feet."[1] Our bodies are a gift, because through our bodies we touch others. Our bodies make relationships possible. Our bodies do much more than simply bearing our minds and spirits.

We care for the body not simply as a support for our head. We are called to care for the body; to stay in shape, so that we may be attuned and open to the call of God in our lives. The great commandment calls us to a balanced life, one that is fully connected in all aspects of our being: mind, body, and spirit. The goal of such care is not merely to attain longevity. It has more to do with the quality of our lives. A quality of wholeness that allows us to be in tune with God's dream for us and, at the same time, to be available to the demands of that dream: to respond to God, to our own needs, and to those of our neighbor's. To be whole is to be balanced, poised to respond. That is why we care for ourselves, so that we may be available to God, to our neighbor, and to ourselves.

Each of these three areas—mind, body, and spirit—can be examined in great detail. Each is the focus of a specific discipline of study. We speak of the mind as encompassing our personality, intelligence, memory, and cognitive function. We speak of our body in terms of gender, proportion, and size, or we focus on areas of pain and dysfunction, or the person that we see in the mirror. We speak of our spirit as sad, happy, joyful, or energized. We can look at each of these areas in almost infinite detail. There are times to look into specific particular areas, but this is not my purpose.

My purpose is to suggest that we draw back the lens and focus on all of who we are. My purpose is to suggest that we focus on our whole body with all its components. If we dwell on details for too long, we cannot see our whole person. We may fail to recognize the connection between body, mind, and spirit. To focus or work on our physical condition affects our mind and spirit. We cannot work on one area without affecting all the others. All aspects—physical and spiritual—contribute to the whole of who we are. Wholeness is not the same as perfection. We are incarnated beings, endowed by God with the gift of life, of our particular genetic makeup, of our family of origin, and of our place in the world. Our bodies are gifts that we are to care for each day if we are to be open to God's call to love.

How do we put into practice our care for the whole life that we are privileged to live? The possibilities seem unlimited. There is so much that we know, and so much we are learning each day. We could study wellness for a long time. We could become very well informed about all dimensions of a healthy lifestyle.

We could spend a great deal of time investigating fitness options. But that very investigation can create another layer of anxiety and concern. Will I make the right choice? Or worse, we put off these possibilities until tomorrow.

In this section I have focused on practice, and that raises the important question of where we begin. We can only begin where we are. We can only take one step at a time. Wellness begins with a walk. We cannot let daunting possibilities for physical activity deter us. We must begin where we are today. Mountains are climbed one step at a time. The Danish philosopher Søren Kierkegaard was an avid walker, "Above all, do not lose your desire to walk. Every day I walk myself into a state of well-being. . . ." Take that first step and put wellness into practice.

In my twenty-six years of practicing family medicine, I have spent a lot of time encouraging healthy lifestyles. I constantly stress the importance of walking. I may not want to walk when it's raining, when it's too hot, when it's too cold. My excuses could go on and on. But if I have learned anything, it is that there really is no good time to do something that we don't want to do.

But we can change if we learn to listen to the spirit moving within us, encouraging us to take care of ourselves. We need God's help if we are to put into practice healthy behavior. We are nothing if not experts in our own resistance to change. Yet, God cares for us and God desires our wholeness, not our perfection. Our bodies are a gift and we must care for them.

That walk to the mailbox or to the corner is a beginning. We can try to walk a little further each day. We can break our walking into smaller distances. Like any change, our natural resistance will show us the disadvantages right away. We won't have to worry about looking for them. They are at the front and center of our thinking. Begin slowly, but begin. Walk, and over time the benefits will become apparent.

Walking benefits our whole person. A weight-bearing exercise, it helps build strong bones and lowers our blood pressure and heart rate. It also lowers blood sugar by making our body's insulin work more effectively. Walking also lowers total bad cholesterol and raises our good cholesterol. Walking reduces joint stiffness and pain over time, improving our mobility. Walking increases our energy. The physical benefits even extend to reducing the risk of many forms of cancer. Persons with cancer who walk experience a twenty percent improvement in survival. Walking boosts immunity and improves sleep. Walking contributes to our ability to be in the present. The result is a life more available to the desires of God.

Walking benefits far more than our physical state. Walking has a way of clearing our heads as we walk. It enhances mental alertness and cognitive functioning. This improved mental acuity enhances our ability to screen out distractions.

Walking supports our emotional and physical well-being. Studies show that the quickest way to improve our mood is by taking a brisk ten-minute walk. Walking, like all forms of exercise, releases hormones in the brain that positively affect our mood. These hormones, called endorphins, act as our body's natural antidepressants. Walking transforms our outlook, reducing anger, depression, and anxiety. John Muir wrote, "I only went out for a walk and finally concluded to stay out till sundown, for going out, I found, was really going in."[2]

I suggest walking because it is so readily available and requires little special equipment. But any exercise has similar results. We know to expect resistance. I am reminded of the "Prayer for Young Persons" from the Book of Common Prayer. The prayer petitions, "Help them to take failure not as a measure of their worth, but as a chance for a new start." (BCP, 829) One of the gifts of our humanity is the gift of failure. We can expect failure, learn from it, and start again. Perhaps ironically, in medicine we know that the person most likely to be successful at implementing a new behavior or dealing with addiction is someone who has tried in the past and failed. The same may be true of exercise and walking. But physical activity strengthens our health in all areas and draws all the parts of our being together into an energized and available whole.

Years ago I began walking at night so that no one would see me. I was self-conscious about exercising. Over time I added other forms of aerobic exercise and resistance training. I began with walking, and it is still the foundation of my exercise. I begin my workouts by walking. I say that walking is to warm up my muscles and that is true, but I really know I do it out of habit. Certainly, during times of vacation, illness, stress, or holidays I have fallen away from my routine. But each time I start back and when I return, I always begin where I began, I walk.

We are not solitary individuals, we are born into community and we are designed for community. Scripture's creation narratives affirm our need for relationship. We find that support helps us, affirms us, and motivates us. Support can be the critical element in making exercise a regular part of our lives. Support can come from a partner, spouse, neighbor, friend, personal trainer, or co-worker. Walking is one of the few exercises that allows conversation throughout the activity. In this way, relationships are strengthened by walking together.

Practice sounds like getting ready for something, like playing an instrument. We are learning and our practice contributes to a balanced life, a life that is whole in body, mind, and spirit. The practice is the regular activity. The practice of healthy living contributes to a healthy life. Practice is also what any student must do, whether it's music, art, dance, or athletics. Practice requires discipline and so does caring for our body by exercising.

Any skill takes practice. Caring for ourselves is no different and requires a lifetime of practice. We are never physically perfect, but perfection is not our goal. Wholeness is not the same as perfection. Wholeness is caring for our body so that we can respond to the opportunities for ministry that come our way. Caring for ourselves makes us comfortable, balanced, and available to and for God. With our body, mind, and spirit in balance we are available to the dream of God to be faithful to God who loves us, created us, and hopes for us. And so we practice, and yes we walk.

☙❦❧

Notes

1. Jean Denton, *Good Is the Flesh* (Harrisburg: Morehouse Publishing, 2005), 129.

2. John Muir, in L.M. Wolfe, ed., *John Muir, John of the Mountains: The Unpublished Journals of John Muir*, 1938.

Emotion Work and Wellness

Elaine C. Hollensbe

If you have the kind of a day where you have dealt with an emergency room situation [and] with a traffic accident, you go to another hospital where you are rejoicing with a family over the birth of their first child. Then you get back to the office where somebody has just written a check for $50,000 to cover the deficit. You know? You can be yanked all over the place [emotionally].[1]

One of the most surprising revelations to emerge in organizational literature in recent years is the recognition that people at work engage not only their heads and hands, but also their hearts. As simple as this idea may sound, research on emotions in organizations is relatively new, appearing only in the past couple of decades. Yet, emotion work is often a part of many occupations. Consider, for example, a store clerk dealing with an irate customer, a nurse counseling a terminally ill patient, or a receptionist greeting a new parishioner. In each of these cases, the job holders are expected to express situationally appropriate emotions, and in some cases, suppress emotions that they actually feel. It would be complicated enough if our work involved only one or two emotions; however, most of us are presented with a range of hassles and uplifts in the course of our work, each eliciting a different emotional response.

For example, I recently had a student visit my office (on the last day of class) concerned about his impending failing grade. Although on the surface I engaged in active listening, internally I experienced increasing frustration that the student had not heeded the syllabus that I had carefully prepared for the course, had not contacted me prior to the last day of class, and was generating a litany of excuses most of which were too far-fetched to believe. As we were talking, I was interrupted by our department secretary reminding me of a budget meeting about to start. Meanwhile, a colleague to whom I am assigned as a mentor, was ringing me on my cell phone asking for advice about her declining course evaluations.

113

All three events occurred within the course of a few minutes, each requiring a different emotional response. In an occupation that ostensibly engages one's mind (professor), it is amazing to me how much of my work actually engages my heart.

This chapter is about emotion work and its implications for wellness. In particular, I discuss two areas of emotion work in which my colleagues and I have completed research—emotional labor and emotion transitions.

Emotional Labor

> Some weddings you are just tickled that this couple is getting married. Other ones you just think, "Lord, you are going to have to do something mighty here." You have to pretend that you are just as excited about both of them. There are also people who you are supposed to act very delighted every time you see them . . . When they walk in, no matter what I am in the middle of, I have to act like I am really happy to see them.

Emotional labor was first defined by Arlie Hochschild in her book *The Managed Heart* as "the management of feeling to create a publicly observable facial and bodily display."[2] It is essentially in the work requirement that we suppress certain emotions and express others. What differentiates emotional labor from ordinary everyday management of emotion is that emotional labor is an expected (though uncompensated) requirement of work. The "intimacy of human emotion is commoditized and literally part of the labor process" rather than just emerging naturally from human interaction.[3] Emotional labor can create dissonance or conflict between emotions we *feel* and the ones we *express*.[4]

Emotional labor can be caused by work requirements, embedded in job-related activities, prompted by particular interaction partners, or required by the situational context.[5] Central to emotional labor is the idea that individuals follow emotional display rules that specify what kind of emotion one should express at work.[6] Display rules are norms about what emotion is appropriate to display, and they "decouple" felt emotion from expressed emotion.[7]

Types of Display Rules

In many cases, researchers have studied one particular type of emotional display rule in their research. For example, they have studied front-line service providers who are expected to express positive emotions and suppress negative emotions;[8] bill collectors who are required to display irritability to motivate delinquent customers to pay their bills;[9] and physicians who must maintain a professional demeanor around patients.[10] Emotional labor at work, however, is often more complex than display rules dictating one particular emotion. With many jobs and vocations, different types of emotional labor are required depending on the particular interaction partner and situation.[11] In our research involving Episcopal clergy, for example, my colleagues and I found that priests often felt required to suppress anger, sadness, anxiety, and happiness; however, they also felt required to express caring, sadness, sociability, and happiness.[12] Display rules can also affect lay people who are expected generally to suppress negative feelings and express positive ones toward the parishioners and staff people with whom they work.

Consequences of Emotional Labor on Wellness

Above all else, guard your heart, for it is the wellspring of life.

—Proverbs 4:23

In general, the literature shows that even though emotional labor can positively affect an organization's performance (e.g., customer satisfaction), it can result in negative consequences for *individuals'* well-being.[13] Individual consequences of emotional labor include emotional exhaustion and stress; mental resource depletion; impaired physical well-being; and burnout.[14] These well-being effects are most noticeable in jobs that have high demand and low control[15] (e.g., customer service representatives) and in jobs involving "people work."[16] However, some researchers have observed positive effects of emotional labor,[17] particularly when felt and expressed emotions become aligned over time and when people become particularly committed to their work.[18] The adverse individual wellness effects occur most often when there is *dissonance* between felt and expressed emotion.[19] For example, dissonance would occur when a lay person is feeling anger but is required to express compassion.

Emotional labor can present even greater challenges when a *variety* of emotions must be displayed.[20] For example, surgical nurses are required to express a range of emotions in their work. On a typical day, they must display warmth (toward patients and families) and a flat, non-anxious demeanor (in the operating room), as well as "true feelings" (with other nurses).[21] Given the variety of emotions we feel and express at work, the *transitions* among diverse emotion demands are important to understand and manage.

Emotion Transitions

I had been in a meeting with some people talking about this program that we are starting that I'm very excited about. I had to turn on a dime and go and have a meeting with a widow whose husband died while I was away this summer. I simply was not prepared for the depth of her pain and grief and sorrow. I really felt the 180-degree turn going on in my psyche. It was a very abrupt change of emotion.

Emotion transitions, which my colleagues and I define as the shifts in emotion associated with changing emotion demands at work, can also involve labor.[22] As the statement above illustrates, work can present many shifting demands, each requiring a different emotion response. Moving among these shifting demands can be challenging due, in part, to what we describe in our research as "temporally mismatched emotions." These lagging and leading emotions complicate the movement from one emotion to another and have wellness consequences.

Temporally Mismatched Emotions

Researchers have studied how emotions travel from person to person as contagion.[23] For example, many of us know from experience that negative (or positive) emotions of a group leader can be "caught" by followers. However, emotions can also travel from event to event. Ideally, the emotions we feel at a given moment are associated with the event or interaction in which we are currently engaged. However, the boundaries between emotions are not always clean separations, and emotions associated with one event sometimes spill over to a new one.

In our research, we found two types of emotion spillover: *recalcitrant or "sticky" emotions* (in which an emotion-charged event ends but the associated emotions do not) and *anticipatory or "tickling" emotions* (in which emotions associated with an upcoming event precede the event). Both cases—recalcitrant and anticipatory—involve a mismatch between a here-and-now emotion and an event, past or future.

Most of the people whom we interviewed in our research reported cases in which they continued to feel recalcitrant or "sticky" emotions from a past event, such as a counseling session with a depressed parishioner or an especially heated vestry meeting. In other words, the emotion persisted long after the event ended:

> Those emotions will come back after everyone else in the house is asleep. Then I'm flipping channels or watching football or just playing the guitar, whatever. Then they all come back and you stare at the ceiling and think it all through some more. I guess it is kind of like I clock out of it, but then I clock back into it, pretty regularly late at night . . . The emotion that is left over comes back late at night.

Nearly half of the people whom we interviewed recounted incidents of anticipatory or "tickling" emotions, which most often included anxiety, fear, or frustration, although a few mentioned positive feelings as well. Like a tickler file, these anticipatory emotions often distract from current activities, but are also sometimes preparatory, as the following quote demonstrates:

> When I get off the phone with you I'm going to go see this fellow at the hospital. So the drive down there I will be changing gears. One of the things I'm thinking about is apparently, just physically, he is all torn up. One of the things I want to do is just to visualize where he is going to be in the ICU, what is he going to look like, what he might be hooked up to. I just try to get in touch with my own anxiety . . . then I check my own self out. Typically I'll say something like, "God, help me . . ." I just try to get centered in my own spirit a little bit.

With both types of temporally mismatched emotions, the boundary between emotions from one event to another is *permeable*. That is, feelings associated with a past or future event can affect a person's ability to engage emotionally in a present event, leading to wellness consequences.

Wellness Consequences of Emotion Transitions

Permeable emotion boundaries and frequent emotion transitions can have a taxing effect, leading to a phenomenon my colleagues and I call *emotion blurring*—a condition in which the swirl of emotions prevents the individual from feeling any particular emotion. Emotion blurring can produce disorientation and an inability to deal with here-and-now emotions. Imagine a fan whirling in which each blade represents an emotion. An observer can detect that there are different blades, but the overall effect is an inability to see one particular blade clearly; the observer is left with only the numbing sense of the overall swirl. As one person whom we interviewed put it, "If you've been from happy to sad to happy to sad so many times that day, you are just not going there again . . . There is just no emotion available." The following quote further illustrates the associated disorientation and confusion associated with emotion blurring.

> Sometimes I'm just like, "How am I supposed to be feeling now?" "What's happening next?" There have been a couple times when you have really stressful days that you are: Should I laugh at this? Should I cry at it? Should I yell at somebody? Should I kick the dog?

Another consequence of emotion transitions that we found was *depersonalization* in which "detachment" (as a strategy to handle interactions and avoid taking on others' emotions) becomes permanent. As a result, a person becomes chronically unable to feel at all, as is illustrated in this quote:

> There are certainly times when I feel like I should be joyful and I'm not really feeling—certainly not joy, and sometimes not even particularly positive feelings at all. Likewise, and maybe more profoundly true for me, and maybe more problematic, is that there are times when I'm trying to help or be with somebody who is really sad, and I just can't feel that. I feel numb . . . I can remember times, having left someone who was grieving significantly, and just sort of being amazed that I couldn't feel anything.

Although emotion blurring and depersonalization are clearly negative consequences of frequent emotion transitions, in our research we found nearly a dozen strategies that individuals reported using to handle these negative effects. In the next section, I describe a few of these strategies to illustrate how emotion work can be managed.

Strategies for Managing Emotion Work

The most common emotion-work strategy, *focusing/immersing*, involves focusing on the particular emotion demand at hand or, as some of the people we interviewed referred to it, being "in the moment." This tactic is, in fact, the *sine qua non* of an emotion transition—to separate oneself cleanly from past or future events and focus oneself squarely and solely on the present event. Although acknowledging multiple emotion demands, the individual in the following quote describes his efforts to remain focused:

> When I'm with the family planning the funeral, I'm with that family. Then again, when I'm with the couple that is getting married, [I am] focusing on them and what their needs are. When everybody is out of the room, then I may jump back and forth between the emotions, but when I'm with people, I just try to focus on just who I am with at that time.

Focus/immersion requires conscious effort to suppress extraneous or unrelated felt emotion. One way to manage this process is through a second emotion-work strategy called *temporally shunting* felt emotion. In this strategy, felt emotions are postponed to a future time, creating essentially a timeline of feelings. For example, a priest at a funeral reported needing to "mourn later" rather than at a funeral, where parishioners "need me to be the priest." By temporally shunting personally felt emotion, individuals can engage more fully in the emotion demands of the present event. One individual likens this shunting to acting:

> There are times like that when you are just plain outside yourself, because there are certain things that need to be done and dealt with . . . You are called upon to lead, be up front, perform, whatever. There is a discipline to that that puts down things that are sort of your own personal emotion. You put that down and you step into the role and you do what you need to do and be in the place that people need you to be in. When you are finished with that, you pick up what you put down and deal with it . . . Every emotion doesn't need to be dealt with in the moment.

Temporal shunting was such a common tactic for managing emotion work among the people we studied that they had developed labels to describe it, such as "bracketing the anger or sadness" they were feeling so that they could lead worship and "compartmentalizing" a felt emotion by "putting it in a place." Once the event had ended, the felt emotion was dealt with in the same way that one would file away a document to be read later.

A third strategy we found for managing emotion work is *reframing*, or identifying the source of or reason for a particular emotion, then reframing the situation to one in which emotions are more manageable. Several individuals reported using reframing tactics to meet emotion demands, often in conjunction with managing difficult parishioners. The next quote illustrates how one individual uses reframing to shift from negative feelings about a challenging parishioner:

> I can think of several examples with her. I didn't feel any kind of positive emotion toward her. I was being very nice, but I just really wanted to shove my fist down her throat or something. When I start feeling that, the thing that helps me the most is to say, not out loud, but looking at that person to say, "You too are a beloved child of God." That helps me through some of the negative feelings that I might have.

Reframing involves representing the person with whom one is interacting in a different (positive) light, lessening the dissonance and work associated with managing emotions.

Emotion Work and Wellness

All of us engage in emotion work throughout our professional and personal lives. Much of the time this work is effortless and, in fact, personally enriching. However, to the extent that there is a mismatch between felt and expressed emotion, or an expectation that we shift emotions facilely from event to event, wellness can be affected. Conscious attention to what are often unconscious processes can help ensure that practicing emotion work yields positive rather than negative wellness consequences.

ᥱᕽᥨ

Notes

1. The quotes in this chapter are drawn from the Borders & Bridges study that my colleagues, Glen Kreiner and Mathew Sheep, and I completed, which was funded in part by CREDO Institute, Inc. We studied Episcopal priests, a population in which emotion, labor, and emotion transitions are frequent. Our research involved open-ended survey responses from 220 Episcopal priests, coupled with in-depth interviews with an additional sixty randomly selected priests. It is important to point out that emotion work extends to many occupations and roles beyond the priesthood, particularly in those involving close interaction with others.

2. A.R Hochschild, *The Managed Heart* (Berkeley: University of California Press, 1983), 7.

3. H.A. Elfenbein. 2007. Emotion in organizations. *The Academy of Management Annals* 1:315–386 (339).

4. S.M. Kruml, and D. Geddes. 2000. Exploring the dimensions of emotional labor: the heart of Hochschild's work. *Management Communication Quarterly* 14:8–49.

5. J.A. Morris and D.C. Feldman. 1996. The dimensions, antecedents, and consequences of emotional labor. *Academy of Management Review* 21: 986–1010; S.J.,Tracy and K. Tracy, 1998. Emotion labor at 911: A case study and theoretical critique. *Journal of Applied Communication Research* 26:390–411; Waldron, V.R. 1994. Once more, with feeling: Reconsidering the role of emotion in work. *Communication Yearbook* 17: 388–416; Schaubroeck, J., and Jones, J.R. 2000. Antecedents of workplace emotional labor dimensions and moderators of their effects on physical symptoms. *Journal of Organizational Behavior* 21:163–183.

6. P. Ekman, 1973. Cross-culture studies of facial expression. In P. Ekman (Ed.), *Darwin and Facial Expression: A Century of Research in Review* (New York: Academic Press, 1973), 169–222.

7. Ibid.

8. A. Rafaeli. 1989. When clerks meet customers: A test of variables related to emotional expressions on the job. *Journal of Applied Psychology* 74:385–393; A.A. Grandey, G.M. Fisk, A.S. Mattila, K.J. Jansen, and L.A. Sideman. 2005. Is "service with a smile" enough? Authenticity of positive displays during service encounters. *Organizational Behavior and Human Decision Processes* 96:38–55.

9. R.I. Sutton, 1991. Maintaining norms about expressed emotions: The case of bill collectors. *Administrative Science Quarterly* 36:245–268.

10. A.C. Smith and S. Kleinman. 1989. Managing emotions in medical school: Students' contacts with the living and the dead. *Social Psychology Quarterly* 52:56–69; H.I. Lief, and R.C. Fox. 1963. Training for "detached concern" in medical students. In H.I. Lief, V.F. Lief, and N.R. Lief (Eds.), *The Psychological Basis of Medical Practice* (New York: Harper Row), 12–35.

11. A. Rafaeli and M.C. Worline. 2001. Individual emotion in work organizations. *Social Science Information* 40:95–123.

12. E.C. Hollensbe, G.E. Kreiner, and M.L. Sheep, Working paper. *Navigating emotion transitions at work.*

13. A. Grandey. (In press). Emotions at work: A review and research agenda. In C. Cooper and J. Barling (Eds.), *Handbook of Organizational Behavior*: Sage.

14. K. Pugliesi, 1999. The consequences of emotional labor: Effects on work stress, job satisfaction, and well-being. *Motivation and Emotion* 23:125–152; J.M. Richards and J.J. Gross. Emotion regulation and memory: The cognitive costs of keeping one's cool. *Journal of Personality and Social Psychology* 79:410–424; J. Schaubroeck, and J.R. Jones. 2000. Antecedents of workplace emotional labor dimensions and moderators of their effects on physical symptoms. *Journal of Organizational Behavior* 21:163–183; D. Zapf. 2002. Emotion work and psychological well-being: A review of the literature and some conceptual considerations. *Human Resource Management Review* 12:237–268; C.M. Brotheridge, and A.A. Grandey. 2002. Emotional labor and burnout: comparing two perspectives of "people work." *Journal of Vocational Behavior* 60:17–39.

15. K. Pugliesi. 1999. The consequences of emotional labor: Effects on work stress, job satisfaction, and well-being. *Motivation and Emotion* 23:125–152.

16. C.M. Brotheridge, and A.A. Grandey. 2002. Emotional labor and burnout: Comparing two perspectives of "people work." *Journal of Vocational Behavior* 60:17–39.

17. S. Cote. 2005. A social interaction model of the effects of emotion regulation on work strain. *Academy of Management Review* 30:509–530.

18. R.H. Gosserand, and J.M. Diefendorff. 2005. Emotional display rules and emotional labor: The moderating role of commitment. *Journal of Applied Psychology* 90:1256–1264.

19. S.G. Barsade, and D.E. Gibson. 2007. Why does affect matter in organizations? *Academy of Management Perspectives* 21:36–59; N.M. Ashkanasy and C.S. Daus. 2002. Emotion in the workplace: The new challenge for managers. *Academy of Management Executive* 16:76–86.

20. J.A. Morris and D.C. Feldman. 1996. The dimensions, antecedents, and consequences of emotional labor. *Academy of Management Review* 21:986–1010.

21. D.R. Denison, and R.I. Sutton. Operating room nurses. In J.R. Hackman (Ed.), *Groups that work (And Those That Don't): Creating Conditions for Effective Teamwork* (San Francisco: Jossey-Bass, 1990), 293–308.

22. E.C. Hollensbe, G.E. Kreiner, and M.L. Sheep. Working paper. *Navigating emotion transitions at work*.

23. Barsade, S.G. 2002. The ripple effect: Emotion contagion and its influence on group behavior. *Administrative Science Quarterly* 47:644–675.

Wellness at Work and Home: Managing Boundaries

Glen E. Kreiner

My wife and I had our first child during my doctoral program. She worked full time during that period of our lives, and so I often took care of our baby daughter during the day. I vividly remember one afternoon in the fall of 1999. I was watching our baby, but had a pressing deadline for a journal article revision. She wanted to be held and would fuss when I put her down. But I needed to write. So, I sat down at my desk, placed her in my lap on a "Boppy" baby pillow, reached over her tiny body, and typed away. A few minutes into this silly scene, the real irony hit me—the article I was writing dealt with a curiously familiar topic—balancing work and family demands!

Each of us—whether we are single, married, or parents—must navigate the pressures between our life domains. For many, the two most demanding life domains are "home" and "work." The purpose of this chapter is to focus on two particular challenges we face in this balancing act, as well as present several tactics we can use to address these challenges.

The Challenges of Work-Home Balance

Individuals differ in their inherent preference to either segment or integrate work and home. Think about your own preference. Do you prefer to keep home at home and work at work? If part of your home life enters your work life, do you welcome it or resent it? Do you mind thinking about work when you're at home? What about the people around you—co-workers, family members, and friends? Do you have a read on their boundary preferences? Are theirs the same or different from yours? What effect does that congruence or incongruence have on you? Boundaries are a lot like international borders: some are well-guarded, while others are open and free; and what works at some times does not work at other times. Maintaining boundaries is a process, and focusing on them thoughtfully can improve them.

Since each person differs in their preferences and expectations about the work-home boundary, we're bound to experience frustrations and disappointments. When the pressures and strains of work and home pile up, we experience "work-home conflict," the generalized state of tension that results from incompatible expectations and challenges associated with work and home.[1] In addition to this ongoing state of conflict, we can also experience particular episodes or events that disrupt our preferred work-home boundary. We call these "work-home boundary violations"—an individual's perception that a behavior, event, or episode either breaches or neglects an important facet of the desired work-home boundary. Work-home conflict and boundary violations can disrupt us on our path to wellness. They have been shown to decrease life, home, and job satisfaction, and increase stress, anxiety, depression, and physiological dysfunctions. They can divert us from the important things in life. The case is particularly problematic for clergy, who have strong demands from their vocation (e.g., availability at all hours, multiple demands on time) as well as family obligations.

Tactics for Boundary Work

Of course, we aren't just interested in knowing the *challenges* of the work-home interface. We are on the lookout for solutions, as well. The good news is that we can do something about the challenges of work-home conflict and boundary violations. In my work with colleagues Elaine Hollensbe and Mathew Sheep, we've identified nine specific tactics that you can employ in order to improve your work-home balance in four categories: cognitive, temporal, physical, and communication. You can also use many of these tactics to help others with their work-home boundary work. These boundary work tactics represent actionable knowledge that can be taught to others for more successful self-management.[2] I invite you to consider how you might apply one or more of them to your current situation, as well as to consider how you might help others by sharing these tactics with them. Further, I invite you to consider how you can work individually and collectively to create a healthy system around you for work-home balance—how might your parish, your family, your church leadership all work together as a system to create a supportive culture and provide the necessary support systems to accomplish a better balance?

Cognitive Tactics

1. *Involving other people.* We're not alone in negotiating the work-home boundary. People such as spouses, children, co-workers, and supervisors can either help or hinder our attempts at work-home balance. We therefore need to think strategically about the role of other people in our own boundary work. One priest described staff members—who could answer phones, intercept in-office visitors, etc.—as a "firewall" of protection from unwanted intrusions. Another priest told his parish administrator not to call him on his day off "unless something is on fire or someone is bleeding from the temples." How might those in your life be able to ease the burden of your work-home demands? How might you ease someone else's burden?

2. *Leveraging technology.* There are several specific ways that we can use technology to help our work-home balance. One priest told us, for example, that he takes his cell phone on vacation in order to be accessible to parishioners (an integration approach) but has his wife answer the phone to ascertain whether the call is important enough to take (a segmentation approach, which also shows "involving other people," the previously mentioned tactic). Several others in our sample mentioned using caller ID to screen calls during non-work hours and giving out their cell phone numbers to only a select few people. One respondent chose to have an answering machine (as opposed to voicemail) so that he could listen to the message while it was being left, and pick up the phone if it was important and/or urgent enough. This was a noteworthy hybrid of segmenting and integrating—the priest wanted to integrate enough to be able to meet parishioners' needs, but wanted the control to segment non-emergencies out of the home. Asking parishioners and staff members to use email instead of telephone calls gave several priests more flexibility as to *when* requests could be met. Some interviewees created separate email accounts: one for personal use, the other for parishioners to use.

3. *Picking and choosing.* We documented ways that an individual can *both* segment and integrate their work and home domains. We call this "picking and choosing" because the individual discriminates about precisely what will or will not pass through the work-home boundary,

as well as which direction (work-to-home or home-to-work) passage is allowed. One area in which this was most evident was that the priests tended to be careful to choose in what aspects of the ministry they involved their spouses and family. For example, many of our interviewees said they do not use family stories or vignettes in their sermons, yet their family members are deeply involved in the work of the church. The difference? In the former case, involvement of family violates family members' volition or privacy, whereas in the latter case, family members choose their involvement. (Interestingly, other priests, however, specifically mentioned how they consciously chose to use those family stories in their sermons, and cited it as a benefit of integrating home with work.) Another example occurring frequently in our data deals with "pastoral emergencies," those crises needing the priest's immediate attention (such as a death or serious accident). These emergencies were often viewed as acceptable exceptions to otherwise strong segmentation norms, making them a kind of trump card to typical boundary management tactics. Interestingly, the aforementioned tactic of invoking triage can be used in tandem with differential permeability; it is often during such crisis modes that individuals make finer-grained distinctions about what can and what cannot puncture the work-home boundary. At the heart of differential permeability is that the individual is consciously choosing which aspects of work and home to integrate, and which to segment, and then acting accordingly.

Temporal Tactics

4. *Controlling work time.* Managing time often becomes crucial to professional success and personal satisfaction. There are several ways that people can control their work time to reduce boundary violations and/or work-home conflict. One approach involved manipulating one's schedule to maximize time with family. This often meant creating and utilizing "blocks" of time that met both work and home schedules' demands. One version of this was for *fairly regular scheduling*, while another dealt with *special occasions* or sporadic but important events. Another common tactic involved "banking" time from one domain to be used later. For example, if a respondent had to work on a night normally reserved for family,

he or she would bank that time and take it out of work time later. This created a temporal equilibrium so that one domain did not suffer (over the long term) at the expense of the other. Flextime programs can facilitate this tactic. Another way that priests controlled their temporal boundaries was in being firm about certain days or hours that they were not working. One noted, "I'm clear about my boundaries at work in terms of when it is my day off. I prefer not to be called, unless it is an absolute emergency and no one else can be reached." Our interviewees also mentioned choosing *when* to perform work tasks, a choice that was viewed as empowering and particularly important in an occupation that is often viewed as "on call 24/7." People's ability to control their work time varies, of course; some professions and circumstances allow for considerable autonomy. If you are not so fortunate, consider how you might be able to at least improve your control: Can you talk with your supervisor or boss to get some wiggle room in the schedule? Can you negotiate scheduling issues before taking a job? Can you integrate this tactic with others, such as involving other people, or invoking triage, in order to maximize your control?

5. *Finding respite.* Taking breaks from work, along with other recovery mechanisms, can have positive benefits for work engagement and overall well being. Our data show that these breaks could ameliorate work-home conflict as well as create a reprieve from the opportunities for boundary violations. Many clergy and lay people have the "two out of three rule"—they will choose two among working mornings, afternoons, and evenings; brief respite can be found during this time. A temporal boundary work tactic we documented dealt specifically with a person's need to remove him or herself from the work domain for a significant amount of time. In our sample, this varied from as little as one or two days to sabbaticals of one year. While at first, one day might not seem like a significant amount, for many of the priests we spoke with, carving out one or two full days seemed to them a difficult task, and one that they sometimes congratulated themselves for achieving. This was particularly evident as later-career priests reflected on their early career stages, noting they had often felt guilty for taking time off from their ministry. Consider the following example of a seemingly simple recommendation from a late-tenure priest:

Pay as much attention to your own stuff as you do to everybody else's. I can tell when I've gone too many days in a row and too many evening meetings and all of a sudden I look at my desk at home and I haven't filed anything or my wife and I haven't gone out or anything. I just know that I have to just say, "No, I'm going to do something different for the next two days, if I can." I think that works for me. It's like an alarm goes off and I say, "No, I've worked for the Lord enough. I'm going to work for me for two days."

Physical Tactics

6. *Adapting physical boundaries.* Physical boundaries, which involve the where of the work-home interface, were often built or used to create a separation of work and home, or dismantled to create integration between work and home. Some priests who lived next to the church created physical barriers between the rectory (home) and the church (work). One priest, who was about to move into a home adjoining the church building, described how she was building a high fence and gate with a garden between the church and the house. She wanted to walk through a "physical barrier" as she went to and from work. In her words:

> Part of the *great* thing is going to be being so close, but part of the *hard* thing is going to be so close, too. So, I wanted to have a place that is private. To do that, the fence that they are going to put up will be a white stockade fence, six feet tall, but the last foot is going to be a lattice top so that there is privacy and some kind of open place at the top. I imagine that we will have some really beautiful gardens. I'm going to buy an arbor that has gates and latticework to grow roses on. It may sound kind of silly, but I really wanted the transition between home and work and back again to be a point of kind of health and beauty. In my imagination, I have climbing roses over the arbor and in the wintertime we will put Christmas lights on it. I really want it to be clear that there is a boundary, but that the passage back and forth is good.

While this example illustrates the *creation* of physical boundaries, several other interviewees in our study described ways that they tried to *reduce* the impact of physical boundaries between work and home. Typically, these priests desired greater integration of their work and home lives, and used the dismantling or lessening of physical boundaries to achieve that goal. For example, several interviewees spoke of inviting parishioners to their homes for socials, dinners, meetings, and parties in order to decrease the boundary between their homes and the church building.

7. *Managing physical artifacts.* Artifacts are visually salient, typically tangible markers that serve as cues for either the work or home domain. Individuals use physical artifacts (often subconsciously) as ways to negotiate the work-home border. The power of the artifacts as cues or signals is shown in this example: "Even my two-year-old knows when I put on a collar that I'm going to a meeting." Some people put all events on one calendar, while others had separate calendars for home and work. Some individuals used one key ring for all doors and functions, while others used separate key rings for work and home. Postal mail was also a physical artifact that some of our interviewees consciously managed, such as by (dis)allowing work-related mail to come to the home.

Communication Tactics

8. *Setting expectations.* The majority of the priests we interviewed found managing expectations to be a helpful technique in balancing work-home demands. One priest commented that parishioners are "looking for a clue from us as to what is appropriate and what is not" and therefore he had "chosen, and very intentionally, to communicate a sense of boundary." Communicating expectations typically meant outlining preferences regarding the work-home boundary to important stakeholders such as a spouse, children, staff members, parishioners, or the vestry. This tactic could involve nuanced signals, or direct conversations or church bulletin announcements, and it involved communication *before* a violation of the work-home boundary had occurred (in contrast to our next code—confronting violators). Several priests discussed including work-home boundary issues as part of their negotiation process in getting their jobs. That is, they made known their

expectations about work-home balance to potential church members and leaders prior to being hired. Generally, the process involved negotiation about particular expectations regarding the work-home interface (e.g., number of hours to be worked each week, the flexibility of those hours). The following example illustrates the importance of sending clear boundary messages as well as the linkage between tactic usage and reduced boundary violations:

> The most important thing, I think, is from the very beginning when you are in a congregation to send the right messages to people. . . . If you establish boundaries quick, like up front, and if you send messages that you want to be truly present to people, but you do not need to be needed, then they don't. There is an ethos or a culture that gets quickly established about where you stand with respect to the whole community and where the boundaries lie.

9. *Confronting violators.* In contrast to the previous tactic of communicating expectations, the tactic of confronting violators occurs *after* a problem has occurred with work-home boundaries. This tactic is used to try to correct what the individual perceives as other people's disregard for an appropriate boundary. The idea is "to communicate with them and try to train them that they need to work around our schedules here, not necessarily expect that we drop everything." Another interviewee said, "Your problem parishioner, you learn to deal with that, and put your arms around that. For some people you've got to set boundaries. You need to say, 'Well, you need to make an appointment and come and see me. At the appointment we will talk about that.'"

Several priests noted that a key part of confronting violators was helping them see that their problem was not urgent. One noted his response to a parishioner who came to his home at night: "I try to say, 'Oh, how long have you had this problem? Okay, you've been drinking for twenty years. Well, how about if we talk tomorrow morning?'" Beyond the more obvious violations such as parishioners or staff calling on one's day off or showing up at the priest's home at inappropriate times, our interviewees reported that they were sometimes faced with having to explain why seemingly innocuous instances were actually work-home violations in their eyes. One priest noted:

When I first came here many people saw me walking my dog or taking walks and several parishioners asked if they could walk with me. Initially, I found that some people were hurt when I said, "No." I had to do a lot of kind of explaining about the importance of time away for me. . . . It was both physical exercise as well as a time for me with God, being alone and outside. It took a lot of education and sometimes hurt feelings and some clear kind of communication about boundaries for me. I think it is pretty well understood, now. Most people understand that and accept it.

Note how the efficacy of this tactic is revealed in the quote: after her intervening and explaining, people understood her preferences and accepted it. In this example, the priest interpreted the parishioners' *requests* to walk with her during her private time as a boundary violation; she framed that private time as bounded and wanted to preserve the boundary. Clearly, not all individuals would frame this episode as a boundary violation, which illustrates the importance of remembering individual differences in your and others' boundary work.

Final Thoughts

Although negotiating the demands between home and work will rarely be easy, the tactics outlined in this chapter can offer support. They have been tested and used successfully. These tactics meld nicely with the CREDO IDPT framework: as we know ourselves better in relation to the work-home boundary, as we discern what is best for us and those we serve, and as we put into practice these boundary work tactics, we can transform our lives both at home and work for their mutual enrichment.

Along with the CREDO Institute, we're on an ongoing journey to better understand how people can better negotiate the demands between work and home. We'd love to hear your success stories about work-home balance, suggestions for others, and any other general comments at bordersandbridges@gmail.com. Drop us a note!

ⵛⵝⵛ

Notes

1. G.E. Kreiner. 2006. Consequences of work-home segmentation or integration: A person-environment fit perspective. *Journal of Organizational Behavior* 27: 485–507.

2. Our framework follows Nippert-Eng's (1996) groundbreaking study on "boundary work." She described how individuals engage in the effort of constructing, dismantling, or maintaining the work-home border via boundary work. C.E. Nippert. *Home and work: Negotiating boundaries through everyday life* (Chicago: University of Chicago Press, 1986).

Permanent Wealth: You CAN Take It with You!

Phyllis T. Strupp

Once upon a time there was a little girl who wanted to play dress-up. She went into her mother's closet and came upon a square purse that looked like a treasure box. She opened it up and it was indeed full of treasure—a wad of twenty-dollar bills! She knew this treasure would make her friends happy, so she went to them and gave away all the bills. Indeed her friends were happy. But her mother was not.

$$\$\$\$$$

As I write this chapter, I am sitting on the porch of our inn at Chautauqua. A woman passing by asks if I'm writing for work or for fun. I tell her "Both." Then she asks what I'm writing about, and I tell her that I am exploring a spiritual perspective on money.

"Oh," she asks, "do you mean the law of universal attraction? How if you think certain thoughts the universe will send money to you?"

(Wow! If it's that easy, why the heck didn't they teach us this in business school?)

"My message is that either you make your money work for you or else you will end up working for it," I tell her.

She gets a shocked look on her face and allows that, yes, most of us probably spend too much time working for our money. Then she hurries off as though I had breathed fire.

Her reaction does not surprise me, nor do I take it personally. After hearing the financial confessions of thousands of people over the past twenty years, I know the question that occupies the human mind with every heartbeat:

How Can I Get MORE MONEY?

When it comes to money, most of us have the mind of a chimpanzee searching for bananas in the jungle. Every fiber of our being is calibrated to the task, and we are thrilled to the core when we get MORE.

You can never be too thin or too rich.

Most people have shared their financial secrets with me because they want one of two things: they want to have MORE MONEY or they want to keep someone else from getting their money.

No one has ever asked for my help in getting rid of money. Nor have I ever heard someone say, "I am rich. I have enough."

How much is enough?

If you have a six-figure household income, you are in the top twenty percent of all U.S. households. A net worth of $1 million or more puts you in the wealthiest five to ten percent of all U.S. households.

However, a million bucks doesn't go as far as it used to. The *Wall Street Journal* says that $5 million is what you need these days to live the kind of lifestyle that the word *millionaire* conjures up.

While the turbulence buffeting the economy as of this writing will affect these statistics, one essential truth remains unchanged: America is a very affluent nation compared to the rest of the world, yet most of us still want MORE MONEY, no matter where the economy stands. It's always a good time to have a little (or a lot!) MORE MONEY.

From everyone who has been given much,
much more will be demanded;
And from the one who has been entrusted with much,
much more will be asked.

—Luke 12:48

Many of the successful people with whom I have worked over the years seemed to have an autonomic sense about handling money. The most common instinctual "financial plan" that I have encountered goes something like this: Get MORE MONEY so there's plenty available when you want or need it. Time is money. Don't put all your financial eggs in one basket. Since life is unpredictable, the only way you can be sure to have enough is to have MORE. Oh . . . and whatever you do, *don't touch the principal!* Then have it all go to the deserving members of your family at your death. And make darn sure the government doesn't get any of it.

Generosity? Humph. That's just a word people use when they're trying to get their hands on MY MONEY.

Legacy? Humph. Legacy involves dying. That's the last thing I want to do. I don't want to hasten that dread day by talking about it and actually making *plans* for it.

Keep watch, because you do not know the day or the hour.

—Matthew 25:13

Most of my clients have been business owners, executives, and professionals—but not *priests*. When I started working with CREDO, I wondered if the clergy would have the same kind of relationship with their money as everyone else.

After meeting individually with dozens of members of the clergy, I've found that indeed they tend to be different from everyone else, in two ways.

Generally they make the same mistakes as everyone else, but they feel ten times worse about it.

And as a group they are attracted to mystery—the mysteries of God, the Trinity, the sacraments. This tendency enables them to tolerate mystery in some other, stranger places—such as their checking accounts and net worth statements.

Some mysteries are meant to be solved.

Overall, my professional experience with a wide variety of people suggests that money has a way of enslaving people and harming mind-body-spirit health and well-being. I have met only a few people who are in charge—their money works for them and enhances their *joie de vivre* and their relationships.

Limbic Logic

For many years, I wondered why it is so easy for even the smartest people to be bossed around by money. Modern finance taught me that it has something to do with fear and greed. However, the two greatest sources of revelation on this topic have proved to be science and scripture.

When it comes to money, evolution has produced in the human species a very strong gas pedal called "emotions" and a very weak brake pedal called "rationality." Scientific findings indicate that the limbic system, the emotional center of the brain, has been evolving in mammals for 225 million years. This small but powerful collection of neurons predisposes all social mammals (especially us!) to explore and exploit opportunities to acquire more resources for ourselves and our familial herd.

So from our limbic system's perspective, doing whatever we need to do to have MORE MONEY makes perfect sense, and is quite "logical."

Limbic logic! Bite, fight, might makes right. Survival of the fittest. Money is power. Go for the gold. Find a way to get MORE MONEY for me and mine.

Limbic logic—it is the wisdom of this world, and it comes naturally to us, welcome or not.

For the wisdom of this world is foolishness in God's sight.
As it is written: "He catches the wise in their craftiness."
                                                              —I Corinthians 3:19

Limbic logic is not logical at all—it's pure emotion, unsupported by the higher cognitive abilities of our more recently evolved cerebral cortex, such as reason, wisdom, and faith. However, the ancient limbic system tends to rule the roost in the human mind. Only through great effort and perseverance can the limbic system be guided and moderated by the frontal lobe—the only part of the brain strong enough to do the job. That's when money becomes the servant, and not the master.

What's amazing is how well the Bible anticipates these scientific findings about evolution and the limbic system, particularly on the topic of money.

After many years of financial education and experience as a financial adviser, it was quite a shock to learn that the Bible has the best advice I've ever read about how to keep the upper hand over limbic logic and make money your servant rather than your master.

Up until about ten years ago, my understanding of the Bible was nil. But as an Education for Ministry mentor for seven years and an avid reader of *Forward Day by Day* and the daily office for ten, I have become more familiar with the Bible.

In the Bible you see what you are looking for . . . and my finance background heightened my interest in what the Bible has to say about money. There are hundreds of references to money and wealth in the Bible, proportionately more in the New Testament.

By and large, the Bible takes a dim view of the pursuit of wealth and the desire to have MORE MONEY, because it comes between us and God and enables the exploitation of what God has made—your own self, other people, and Nature.

The Old Testament clearly stakes out the spiritual challenges that limbic logic creates for us in these passages:

By your great skill in trading you have increased your wealth,
and because of your wealth your heart has grown proud.
                                                              —Ezekiel 28:5

Whoever loves money never has enough;
Whoever loves wealth is never satisfied with his income.
This too is meaningless.

—Ecclesiastes 5:1

In the 2,500 years since these passages were written, things haven't changed much. As Christians in America today, we still have our work cut out for us when it comes to limbic logic. Here we are, wired by millions of years of evolution to want MORE MONEY, living in a rich country obsessed with having MORE MONEY, and upholding a tradition that warns us that we cannot serve both God and money.

This conflict between the values of our culture and our tradition regarding wealth creates psychic tension in Episcopal parish life, particularly during stewardship season.

One November Sunday a few years ago, a wealthy businessman, the husband of a friend, made one of his rare appearances at church and was treated to an especially heavy-handed stewardship sermon. It sounded something like this: You need to have LESS MONEY so we can have MORE MONEY.

At the coffee hour, the husband made a beeline for me. "Phyllis, I want to ask you something. Over the years I have heard repeatedly at church how bad money is. If money is so bad, why is it that every time I come to church they are trying to get some of mine?"

On another occasion, another wealthy businessman came up to me at coffee hour. "Phyllis, do you know the Golden Rule?" I could tell by the twinkle in his eye that he did not mean the one I was thinking of, so I bit. He chuckled, "The one with the gold makes the rules!"

Limbic logic is ubiquitous in America today, even at church, where it is least expected. Yet we've been shown a better way.

Jesus understood limbic logic very well. He had his own struggles with it, especially during his desert sojourn before he began his ministry. Throughout the Gospels, Jesus rises above limbic logic at every turn, channeling it into the more evolved ways of thinking and living that God graciously wills for us.

Growing Rich Toward God

In Luke 12:21, Jesus points out that when it comes to worldly wealth, the name of the game is to grow "rich toward God." It's OK to have money—if it helps you grow rich toward God. And worldly wealth includes something worth more than your money: your time.

Time isn't money. Time is life.

So how do you grow rich toward God?

Just as we are very attached to our own families, God is very attached to the divine family—which is pretty big. The divine family includes the whole universe—the stars and planets, the earth and its resources, and all the living species (human and nonhuman) that share the earth. Every atom and molecule in Creation is part of the divine family—including our money!

Genesis, generate, generous, generativity . . . all from the Latin word *genus*, meaning descent or birth.

Whoever decided to make our money green knew what he (she) was doing. Green is the color of life, and God is the author of life. In your hands, the power of money is the power to generate new life.

Generate new life in the divine family to grow rich toward God.

Now the cool thing about using money and time to grow rich toward God is that these forms of wealth become permanent and last beyond death, as Jesus assures us in Luke 16:9:

I tell you, use worldly wealth to gain friends for yourself, so when it is gone, you will be welcomed into eternal dwellings.

So when it comes to money, you *can* take it with you, if you use it to grow rich toward God by affirming the life God has placed within you and around you.

How does growing rich toward God look? Here are some examples.

An affluent woman I know became a grandmother several years ago. She was struck by the gifts that were showered on her daughter through the kindness of friends and family. She wondered about all those women who give birth and receive no gifts. In her quiet way, she launched a new ministry that allows her to give hundreds of baby blankets and clothes to indigent women having babies at a local hospital.

A young woman I know lives in a ritzy neighborhood right up against a rocky mountain. One day she found a baby javelina (a wild desert animal that looks like a pig) in her back yard, alone, shivering, and vulnerable to predators. She took it to an animal rescue shelter, where they nursed the baby back to health and placed it in a new herd. She was so affected by their caring work that now she volunteers at the shelter once a week, cleaning pens so the full-time staff has more time to help save animals at risk.

An affluent man I know is a hospice volunteer. He had a patient who was 103 years old, who wanted to talk about God. She told him that she had gone to the Episcopal Church her whole life, but never really felt it inside. As they talked, she shared her views on God and what happens after death. She told him that in talking to him she finally felt it inside, and she died a peaceful death three weeks later.

These stories show us that when it comes to growing rich toward God, it's not just about time and money, and it's not just about writing checks to worthy causes. It's about giving your heart to something—and then any amount of time or money you also give is compounded through the love of God.

A kind heart wielding time and money to grow rich toward God builds permanent wealth.

At this point, chances are you would like to have your cake and eat it too. So how do we get MORE MONEY and grow rich toward God at the same time? Our innate tendency toward limbic logic makes this a very difficult task, since it inclines our hearts to put money above God, just as the Bible warns. To be successful, you need two things: an organization chart and a "well-th" plan.

The organization chart is easy. You work for God, and your money works for you. There are dotted lines between you, other people, and the natural world: they don't report to you, but you have a relationship with them. That's the chart laid out for us in the Genesis story of Adam and Eve.

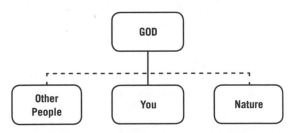

Once you have those relationships down, it's time to develop a "well-th" plan—something very different from the innate, autonomic financial plan we discussed earlier.

The "Well-th" Plan

The goal of a "well-th" plan is to ensure that time and money are spent in life-affirming ways that are meaningful to both you and your boss (God). The successful "well-th" plan will have four parts: physical fitness, mental fitness, spiritual fitness, and fiscal fitness.

Heed the counsel of the CREDO health faculty in other chapters of this book on how to take good care of your body and mind, because it is difficult to be life-affirming to others if you are not generative to yourself.

For God's sake, whatever you do, do not be the cause of your own illness.

—The Cloud of Unknowing

Your brain is part of your body and mind, and a fit, growing brain will help you gain wisdom throughout life—wisdom about God, relationships, and money—as you strengthen your frontal lobe and avoid cognitive decline. A brain that is wealthy in terms of the synaptic connections that underlie wisdom is something money can't buy.

Make sure that money doesn't keep you awake at night, because a good night's sleep is one of the most brain-healthy gifts you can give yourself. At a CREDO conference, one participant shared this anecdote: "My bishop said that anyone who can't get a good night's sleep is a damn fool, because he or she doesn't know enough to let God run the world for at least eight hours a day."

If you are going to report to God and be the boss of your money, your "well-th" plan also needs to include a daily spiritual discipline to train your mind to check in with God, and to see how God is at work within you and around you. Yes, you need a discipline. Thanks to limbic logic, this awareness will not come instinctively at this particular point in the evolution of our species. If you have a discipline, you'll know when you are off track. And the spirit is the strongest part of a person—a little bit of training goes a long way in helping make one healthy in mind and body and a master of money.

Spiritual fitness requires reflection on the meaning and purpose of your life. What is God up to, how do you fit in, and how can your heart, time, money, personality, and best efforts be engaged to further God's work in the world? What can you do to help the other living creatures around you survive and thrive? What are your passions and priorities—that's where meaning lives.

Now you are ready for the part of the "well-th" plan that has to do with getting MORE MONEY as you grow rich toward God.

Fiscal fitness results when the power of counting is wielded to balance opposing forces and build permanent wealth: cash in and cash out, assets and debts, credits and debits, risk and return—all are nothing more than a means of achieving your goals.

Most people have a natural inclination to focus on one force more than the other. For example, Ebenezer Scrooge is asset-minded, joyless, and too focused on saving, while the Prodigal Son is debt-minded, profligate, and too focused on spending.

To hoard or to be bankrupt? That is the question.

Scrooge needs more passion and compassion; the Prodigal Son needs more accountability and self-restraint.

There's no mystery to accumulating money. Spend less than you earn, save money, avoid debt, insure against disasters, minimize taxes, use dollar-cost averaging, and diversify investments across the four asset classes of cash, bonds, stocks, and real estate in a manner consistent with your goals, risk tolerance, and time horizon. Avoid panic selling. If you invest properly, your assets should increase in most years, regardless of market conditions.

When it comes to budgeting, this is what matters:

1. Budget your savings, and save by electronic transfers from a paycheck or checking account to an investment account.

2. Keep meaning and spending in line. Spend money in ways that are generative and joyous for yourself and others, especially your spouse, children, and other immediate family.

3. Figure out a repayment plan *before* you incur a debt.

To be fiscally fit, perform a checkup at least once a year to see whether your net worth is growing or shrinking, and to confirm that it is in line with your permanent wealth goals. Add up the numbers and learn from them. They will speak to you honestly and without judgment. Listen to them—especially if they have bad news for you. This is the easiest, quickest way to come to your senses and get back on track with your "well-th" plan!

If money truly *isn't* important to you, give it all away, take a vow of poverty, and join a Franciscan community. If you aren't quite ready for that, money *is* important to you. So be a good steward of it.

She who is faithful with little is faithful with much.

Everyone makes mistakes with money, fumbling around to find the balance between too much and too little discipline. If you make a mistake, pull back, have a desert experience, and empty the clutter and limbic logic from your mind. Learn your lesson and move on; don't castigate yourself and compromise your wellness and your relationships.

Every dollar of income and expense, asset and debt, is a blessing to you that can teach you how to grow rich toward God.

As you accumulate MORE MONEY, be careful: You are at risk for all kinds of spiritual infections. The most virulent one is the idea that you deserve your money due to hard work, smarts, or some other characteristic unique to incredible, wonderful you.

There are billions of people in the world—also members of God's family—who work very hard and have little or no money to show for it. Hard work by itself entitles you to nothing. Luck and grace play a role in determining who has money.

> The race is not to the swift or the battle to the strong,
> nor does food come to the wise
> or wealth to the brilliant or favor to the learned;
> but time and chance happen to them all.
>
> —Ecclesiastes 9:11

We are all stewards, not owners, of worldly wealth. Everything visible in the world—every cell in your body, every hair on your head, and every dollar in your portfolio—comes from the same clump of atoms and molecules that burst forth 14 billion years ago from the Big Bang through the word of God and the mind of Christ. And it is all going back to God as well—hopefully enriched by the journey.

Now your "well-th" plan is ready for action. As you live into it, may you become more whole and rich toward God as you accumulate MORE MONEY and build permanent wealth.

> All things come of thee O Lord, and of thine own have we given thee.
>
> —I Chronicles 29:14b

Living My Legacy

Now in case you haven't guessed, I was the little girl who gave all those twenties away in the opening story. I was five years old, and the year was 1963, so $20 was a *huge* amount of money, which would buy a lot of penny candy.

When I told my mother what I had done, she immediately called the parents of my friends and asked them to return the twenties. In turn each said, "Gee, little Johnnie and Susie didn't bring home any stray twenties. I'm sorry I can't help you."

Fortunately my mother wasn't mad at me, nor was I punished. I remember that she was upset with the parents for not returning any of the money—not one twenty came back to her.

But what I remember most is that feeling . . . the pure joy of finding the treasure and giving it away to my friends without any hesitation! It never even occurred to me to keep one of the twenties for myself.

The legacy passed at death does not help me grow rich toward God because there is no joy in the giving. I have to give it away wisely to the divine family *while I'm alive* to build permanent wealth and take it with me! I have to live my legacy and pass it along through the instrument of a grateful heart rather than a skillfully executed will.

I work for God, my money works for me, and I am living my legacy!

May my "well-th" plan allow me to give away my own money with the same freedom and joy with which I gave away my mother's money so long ago.

> Why spend your money on what is not bread,
> And your labor on what does not satisfy?
> Listen, listen to me, and eat what is good,
> And your soul will delight in the richest of fare.
>
> —Isaiah 55:2

Permanent wealth is the richest of fare.

TRANSFORMATION

How Am I Changing?

Life is not a series of events to be controlled. Life is a way of walking through the universe whole and holy.

—Joan Chittister

As we shift from practice to the fourth stage of the identity cycle, transformation, we confront the open-ended question, "How Are We Changing?" Managing change is a constant challenge and directly informs, reforms, and perhaps transforms our sense of identity. You may be familiar with the old saying that change is inevitable but choice is always an option. The essays in this chapter explore various perspectives of change and the choices we can make to manage our lives and live into a greater sense of wholeness and well-being.

Drs. Hollensbe, Kreiner, and Sheep explore the concept of "Fit" in "Fitting Square Pegs into Round Holes. . . ." Becoming more aware of congruence and incongruence with others and with organizations can lead us to opportunities for positive growth and wellness.

The Rt. Rev. Mark Hollingsworth challenges us in his essay, "Fitness for God's Mission," to address two open-ended questions: How are we fit for God's mission?" and "To what degree we are up to the challenges of ministry before us?" We find that our capacity to serve others and fulfill God's mission depends in large part upon the disciplines we practice which can ultimately transform our lives.

In their essay, "Transforming 'Growing Pains' into 'Identity Gains,'" Drs. Kreiner and Sheep describe four tactics for identity growth that may facilitate positive change, acknowledging that there's no guarantee that all change is good.

The Rev. Brian Taylor lifts up the hope of transformation in his essay claiming that we are on a Christian pilgrimage calling us to change, grow, and ultimately, to be transformed. He suggests that our Christian transformation consists of a mysterious interplay of human effort and divine grace.

Dr. Elaine Hollensbe begins her essay with the wonderful image of the "little engine that could" to capture the essence of the social science theory, self-efficacy. The belief in one's ability to engage in a task or change, and readiness to change, can radically impact and even transform our sense of well-being. She offers interesting ideas and practices to strengthen our self-efficacy so that we can move from "I think I can" to "I knew I could."

As an avid fly-fisherman, Barton T. Jones shares his personal experiences in fishing as a wonderful metaphor for seeking his soul—an ongoing, enriching pursuit that has been transformative and life-giving.

"Fitting Square Pegs into Round Holes" and Other Challenges of Fit and Wellness

Glen E. Kreiner
Elaine C. Hollensbe
Mathew L. Sheep

If you choose the wrong person for the job, you shouldn't be surprised if they are melting down ten years later. It's no shame on the person who is melting down. It is just that they were a square peg that was put in a round hole.[1]

I can't expect as a priest not to get hurt. I struggled with getting hurt, particularly in [my last parish]; it was a very difficult place for me. They finally asked me to leave. That parish was a bunch of downers. I'm an upper. I think personally it just wasn't right, as I look back on it. For the first time in my life, I discovered I was really nice to people and I thought they liked me. Well, of course they didn't. I've discovered that even the Lord Jesus Christ himself had to be crucified on earth. Even God had to be crucified, who loves human beings. When you love other human beings, you are going to experience pain.

What Is "Fit" and Why Should We Care?

"Fit," as used broadly, refers to the congruence or compatibility between a person(s) and another entity or their environment. Attitudes, values, skills, abilities, and expectations are examples of what might provide the basis for congruence. As illustrated in the quotes above, an individual can experience different levels and types of fit with his or her environment. Most of us, when we reflect for a moment, can recall contexts (jobs, ministries, memberships, social situations, and so on) in which we enjoyed

147

the pleasures of blissful congruence between "who we are" and a particular context. Unfortunately, many of us have also experienced the pain and stress that unintentional or unexpected incongruence can produce (as in the second quote above). Fit matters.

The basic premise of fit is that a match between an individual and his/her environment will yield healthy results, whereas a mismatch will produce unhealthy ones. In fact, research has shown that fit is typically associated with positive outcomes such as increased satisfaction, commitment, performance, and pro-social behaviors, whereas misfit is associated with negative outcomes such as stress and burnout.[2] Clearly, congruence between an individual and his or her environment has its attractive features: it enables the individual to function efficaciously and harmoniously in his or her social world as an integrated, whole, coherent, competent individual. Yet, the reality is that most individuals are at least *somewhat* at odds with various aspects of their environment, whether that be at home, at work, at church, or other domains of one's life. Hence, an understanding of the types of fit and how to manage them is important. In this chapter, we therefore examine (1) what kinds of fit are pertinent to individuals, groups, and organizations; and (2) how to use fit and misfit as opportunities for personal and systemic growth.

Fit with What and Whom?

In our research on Episcopal clergy, leadership, and laity, we have found several ways that individuals might or might not fit with other individuals and groups. Let's take a quick look at these. For each one, consider how it applies to yourself and those around you.

1. *Person-group fit* refers to congruence between an individual and an important group with which he or she deals. In the context of ministry, this often manifests itself as a clergy member's fit with groups such as the vestry or the congregation as a whole. Several clergy members in our research have told us stories of parishioners expecting the priest to be available "24/7" (even during vacations) for all situations, emergency or not. Conversely, others noted that finding a congregation that respected their boundaries and other preferences was a welcome relief, as illustrated in this example:

   > When I was interviewing, my two-year old got deathly ill with croup and had to be hospitalized down here. I just ended the

interview. I just said, "Good-bye, I'm now a mom." I thought that was the end of my career in this parish because I just so definitely said, "I can't talk to you anymore. I really have to see what is happening with my daughter." They were really wonderful. They were very eager to make it work. When I would say to them, after we got down here, "I thought that you would never call me after that, that it was sort of the exhibition of your worst fears about calling a woman with small children," they said, "No, it was really clear to us that you had your priorities in order." I just told them, "This is how it is and we will talk in a couple weeks, but right now I have to do this." They really were wonderful.

As with all forms of fit, person-group fit can also apply to a lay person engaged in ministry. Lack of fit can lead to similar wellness consequences to those discussed earlier, such as fatigue, stress, and burnout.

2. *Person-superior fit* refers to congruence between an individual and his or her superiors. As examples, some priests had head rectors who, because of their own preferences, expected the priests working for them to do things that violated the priest's own expectations, such as: (1) place his or her home phone number in the weekly bulletin; (2) have his or her spouse attend all church and social functions; (3) be available for appointments even on days off; and (4) rearrange his or her schedule on the whim of parishioners. One priest noted of his superior, "He doesn't respect [my] boundaries . . . He doesn't buy into it. . . . He sees that as a sign of laziness more than anything." Another told us:

> I would say that I have a different style and I am accustomed to a different style of leadership than the rector that I work for here has. Because of who I am, sometimes it is hard for me to remain respectful of the fact that his style is simply different, not better or worse, than anybody else's style. As a result, I can get very frustrated with the way that he makes decisions. That can get me sort of heated and frustrated and feeling very spent because I will go off and just kind of try to pay attention to my ministry and do my work and he will do something that in some way undermines, even though he doesn't mean to, what it is that I am trying to accomplish. That is frustrating.

3. *Person-staff fit* is found when a person feels congruence with the staff people he or she supervises. Lack of fit occurs when a person is at odds with his or her staff in terms of certain attitudes, beliefs, or expectations. One example of *in*congruence was given by an interviewee who told us, "My administrative assistant . . . is always buzzing me about this, that and the other thing . . . that he could write up and wait until I get back to the office. . . . He's the one most likely to interrupt me or annoy me at home." In cases in which there is a persistent lack of fit between a person and his or her staff, there can be both physical and emotional wellness consequences for the individual experiencing the incongruence, as well as for the staff. This suggests the need to include some form of screening during hiring, as well as the ability to provide feedback to staff members when needed regarding expectations and their possible violations.

4. *Person-occupation fit* refers to the congruence between an individual and the typical demands of that individual's occupation. The general consensus among priests we interviewed is that the priesthood as an occupation places unique demands on them, which often creates incongruence between how they perceive their true selves and what the calling demands of them. As one priest noted, "I do think the priesthood is unique because you stand up in front of an altar and in front of God on two separate occasions, and you promise you'll put this thing first in your life: one is when you are married and one is when you are ordained." At the same time, priests and lay people may find themselves engaged in ministry in which there is a lack of fit between their skills and abilities and those required by the role.

We found that person-occupation fit can manifest itself in two ways. First, a fairly global fit can occur, with the person perceiving that their whole self is congruent with the demands of the occupation or role. As one interviewee put it, "I think there is a good marriage or a good meeting between who I am and the vocation." Second, a more idiosyncratic or selective fit can occur, wherein the individual identifies certain *aspects* of themselves that fit better than others. For example, one rector told us, in response to a question about whether there were times he couldn't be his true self (thus producing some degree of emotional labor and increased stress):

> Yeah, a lot of times. I have to temper my exuberance. I tend to be sort of in your face. That's just the way I am. I tend

to be high spirited and I like to laugh. I've had to learn that sometimes that is difficult for people. Sometimes they want me to be a little bit more sober in situations. So, I've had to recognize that there are friends and people that you can just be yourself with. I don't think I work too hard at trying to do that. That's one of the reasons that I chose the parish that I am in because I felt like I could be who I was here. I was at a very large, affluent parish before. I felt constrained at times.

When individuals experience this more selective kind of fit, the challenge is to be able to integrate those aspects of themselves (such as skills, personality dimensions) that best serve others, while not getting too frustrated with restraining those aspects that don't fit as well. As one priest told us, "I'm working on [a plan] now of really sort of making a plea to the leadership of the congregation to let me do the stuff that I'm good at, to let me do the stuff that will integrate the best aspects of my priesthood for the good of this parish."

Fit and Misfit as Opportunities for Growth

Most individuals will find fit on some dimensions of life and misfit on other dimensions. Therefore, we find it fruitful to examine *both* the circumstances of congruence *and* incongruence to show how individuals can leverage either situation for growth. In short, congruence provides safety for some types of growth within a safe harbor (fosters growth), whereas incongruence provides opportunity for dynamic tension to spur growth (springboard for adaptation, change, growth). For example, in the context of ordained ministry, seminary training and internships often provide valuable learning and experience that may serve as leading indicators of person-occupation fit. Moreover, internships or prior life experience may help to sensitize people in all sorts of ministry to ways that person-group fit can both manifest itself and be effectively managed. In both types of fit, and whether the experiences are initially negative or positive, using them as triggers for personal growth and development is key.

To best understand how an individual might leverage the state of congruence, it is instructive to first draw the distinction between two types of fit that research has uncovered: complementary and supplementary fit. *Complementary fit* is achieved when an individual has some skill, talent, or ability that is necessary but lacking from the group or organization.

The individual is the proverbial "odd man out," yet can be valued because he or she brings to the table something that the group did not previously have. In a complementary fit situation, growth can occur as the individual learns from others in the group who have skills and abilities that are not currently held by the individual. This growth can be tied to identity such that the newly acquired skills actually change identity, or relationships are improved with those giving/receiving the skills.

Unlike complementary fit, *supplementary fit* occurs when the individual has some aspect that is redundant and compatible with group members. As one rector told us, "one of the things I say frequently in this congregation is that I have felt more able to be myself here than any place else I've ever served." The opportunity for growth is somewhat harder to perceive in this context, as we tend to see growth as stemming from challenges or adversity. However, in the context of supplementary fit, the individual has an opportunity to work from a "safe haven" to try other approaches to growth. That is, because of the generally safe condition of being with like-minded company, the individual can engage in taking on possible selves or better weather identity threats that come along. We also note that there's a potential downside to extreme supplementary fit—if everyone in the group (whether that be a congregation, vestry, or workgroup) is pretty much the same, while they might fit well together, it works against diversity of perspective and may produce negative in-group biases, insular thinking, and/or flawed decision making (such as groupthink).

Finally, let's consider states of *incongruence*, which occur when the values of the individual do not align with those of the group or organization. We suggest that incongruence offers the opportunity for identity growth via two processes, what we call "adaptation-staying" and "learning-exiting." In the *adaptation-staying* process, the individual changes in order to fit with his or her environment and therefore, after adapting, stays with the group or organization. In this process, the opportunity for growth mirrors the complementary fit scenario above, wherein the individual can grow by adopting new skills, abilities, or attitudes. For example, a priest we interviewed told us that when she first arrived at her parish, she didn't fit well with the lay leaders in the congregation, leading to contentious meetings; but that over the years "there has been movement and growth" among them. Another priest told us:

Most of what a priest is called upon to do, does not come sort of easily to me. I'm a bit of an introvert. So I've had to do a lot of growing in order to grow into the sort of gregarious role that I think people expect from their clergy. So, that is one disconnect. It's not me being this happy-go-lucky fellow who is full of energy and is constantly bubbly with people. That takes an effort to do that. If I had my druthers, I'd probably be like most Episcopalians: I'd sit in the back row and say my prayers quietly. . . . I feel like I've conformed and molded myself into a pretty well-adjusted example of what is needed in a priest. So therefore it feels like, yes, a lot of formation.

In seeking to adapt to match the expectations of their profession or role, individuals can make changes in their identity to fit work demands. In doing so, they may be more likely not only to stay in the current context but also to thrive in it, achieving a more congruent sense of "who one is" in that particular context.

In contrast, sometimes adaptation is not a viable option. Perhaps identity change would mean an undesirable change in values, or too great a personal sacrifice. As one of our interviewees told us, trying to change too much is "like squeezing blood out of a turnip. I'm trying. It just doesn't work because that's not who I am." Therefore, instead of changing, in the *learning-exiting* process, the individual decides to exit the group or organization because of the incongruence experienced, but has the opportunity to learn about oneself from the process (such as through the contrast effects with others in the parish, diocese, or vestry; or through self-reflection about mistakes made in joining the organization). Of course, individuals too often deny themselves this reflection and learning opportunity, instead blaming the situation or other individuals involved.

In sum, regardless of the situation—incongruence or congruence—an individual has the opportunity to leverage it for growth. This enables individuals to frame either kind of situation as a growth opportunity.

Concluding Thoughts

We would encourage clergy, lay leaders, and parishioners to consider their individual investment in fit, as well as the more systemic and cultural issues of fit in their parishes and dioceses. How would you describe the fit situation where you are? What is working and what is not? And how can you leverage various forms of fit *and* misfit for the maximum growth and wellness of yourself and those around you? Because of the many levels wellness engages, fit is a useful framework as it, too, crosses levels, meaning fit applies to relationships between individuals, between individuals and groups, and between individuals and organizations. Also, it is important to understand fit because of its relationship with a host of important individual (e.g., stress and burnout) and organizational (e.g., commitment and performance) outcomes. In sum, sensitivity to how well "pegs" and "holes" fit together can lead to positive wellness consequences for individuals, groups, and the organizations in which they work.

ℰℵℭ

Notes

1. In this chapter, we include several quotations that derive from our "Borders and Bridges" research project, which was funded in part by CREDO Institute. It was based on interviews with 60 Episcopal clergy. We also draw on our "Episcopal Identity Project," which was funded in part by CREDO Institute and the College for Bishops. This project was based on data from a variety of sources and populations.

2. For a summary, see A.L. Kristof. 1996. Person-organization fit: An integrative review of its conceptualizations, measurement, and implications. *Personnel Psychology* 49:1–49.

Fitness for God's Mission

Mark Hollingsworth, Jr.

Elite athletes from around the world traveled to Beijing to represent their nations in the 2008 Summer Olympics. After months and years of disciplined training, each was preparing to reach the peak of competitive fitness during the middle two weeks of August. The ability to perform effectively in their respective sports is the product of carefully followed physical, nutritional, emotional, and spiritual disciplines that come together in a holistic integration, a fitness for athletic endeavor that matches the particular challenge of each event.

Of course, some element of success is related to natural gifts and ability. Michael Phelps, who has won more Olympic gold medals than any other human being, began with a natural talent for swimming that was identified by his coach, his mother, and himself when he was a boy. In discerning a vocation to swim competitively, his vision of and passion for excelling in the sport matured. Through the endless practice of disciplines that focused his spirit, developed his muscles, and refined his performance, he began an ongoing transformation that rendered him fit for his task. For Phelps and other athletes, identity, discernment, and practice all contribute to a continuing transformation that results in fitness.

Perhaps more illustrative than Phelps is Dara Torres, five-time Olympian and mother of a two-year old, who at the age of forty-one swam in three events in Beijing, winning the silver medal in each. Her Olympic career spanning almost a quarter of a century (1984–2008), Torres has clearly pursued a continually developing fitness for competitive swimming. During that time her identity has evolved, her body has aged, her metabolism has changed, and her vocational focus has developed to include television commentator, print model, and parent.

In answering the call to serve God's mission, Christians are challenged to a fitness that is likewise the product of an ongoing transformation, a conversion into what we discern God may be dreaming for us to become. It begins with our identification with the person and ministry of Jesus. That identity is developed through a process of discerning how our particular Christian vocations might be manifested as we imagine and explore what it means for us to be Christian. By the practice of worship, prayer,

155

study, and service we grow and are transformed into new life, maturing bit by bit into what St. Paul called the full stature of Christ.

When we hear the term *fitness for mission*, we may think in terms of a narrow measure of moral purity. This is a mistake. When we ask, "Am I fit for God's mission?" we should not be questioning whether we are worthy of it but whether we are up to the task. Of course, none of us is by our own nature so worthy. It is by God's grace alone that each of us is invited into the ministry of Jesus. Indeed the gift of ministry is given to each of us as a journey by which we become more godly. Through our various ministries as lay and ordained Christians, God draws us deeper into God's heart and forms us in the image of Christ. Fitness for those ministries, as with the fitness of an athlete, results from the continual integration of a range of practices and disciplines. It is an ongoing process of growth in Christ that hinges on increasing self-awareness (Identity), grasping a vision of what God is offering us (Discernment), undertaking the disciplines that will realize that vision (Practice), and giving ourselves to the conversion to which they lead (Transformation).

In practical terms, fitness for God's mission has to do with our ever-developing capacity for compassion, honesty, generosity, humility, gratitude, and surrender. It has to do with our ability to take the "other" into ourselves, no matter who that may be, to the end that we might become more whole ourselves. It has to do with our creativity in response to the broken world around us. Furthermore, it has to do with the faithful nurture, maintenance, and stewardship of the assets God gives us in order that we might do ministry: our bodies, our relationships, our personal and financial security, and the realities of the contexts in which we serve. All of these inform our self-awareness, our vocational discernment and vision, the spiritual disciplines and faith practices we employ for our growth, and thus our transformation into what God is making of us.

One of the gospel stories that well illustrates this transformation is the account of Jesus and the Canaanite woman, who sought Jesus' healing ministry for her daughter. On the surface, it appears to be about the woman's fitness to receive Jesus' attention. She persistently follows him and his disciples, publicly appealing to Jesus to heal her daughter, shouting, "Have mercy on me, Lord, Son of David; my daughter is tormented by a demon." The disciples are intolerant, as apparently is Jesus, whose initial response is dismissive, likening her to a dog. In judging her fitness to receive his ministry he tells her, "It is not fair to take the children's food and throw it to the dogs." But then something happens. The woman of

Cana, socially inferior to and ethnically other than Jesus and his disciples, pleads again for her daughter while not contesting the social realities of her situation, replying, "Yes, Lord, yet even the dogs eat the crumbs that fall from their masters' table." And Jesus is changed. Matthew's gospel reports, "Then Jesus answered her, 'Woman, great is your faith! Let it be done for you as you wish.' And her daughter was healed instantly."

The story must be understood as being about Jesus' transformation. Its focus is not ultimately on the Canaanite woman's fitness to receive for her daughter Jesus' ministry of healing, but on Jesus' own increasing fitness for ministry, his increasing fitness for God's mission of love. Its central focus is Jesus and his self-understanding: "I was sent only to the lost sheep of the house of Israel." As a story about both his humanity and his divinity, and about the transformation resulting from his practice of compassion, it is a model for our own transformation, our own conversion to godliness, our own ever-developing fitness for God's mission. Jesus' identity, his self-awareness as healer and minister of God's love, was informed by this pleading mother, whose persistence revealed less about herself than it did about him and his divine vocation. And Jesus' spiritual practices of listening and compassionate attention, of making room in himself for her, increased his awareness of who he was to be to her. It resulted in a change of heart, a transformation, becoming in his humanity more fully who he was in his divinity. Regardless of how each of us might imagine Jesus' messianic consciousness, in Matthew's story his identity is informed and his ministry transformed by his encounter with this woman who believed in him. Her persistent appeal pushed Jesus to engage spiritual and vocational muscles that needed to be stretched.

You and I have practices—physical, spiritual, emotional, and vocational—that make us increasingly fit for God's mission. Disciplines of prayer, of worship, and of service. Disciplines that define us as disciples of Jesus. Disciplines that can transform us into what we have discerned God is patiently and persistently trying to make of us, and sometimes into what we had never imagined God was offering. God gives us the church, at its best both a supportive community for our growth and one that challenges our security with the diversity and conflicting differences God calls into it. In addition, God gives us the gift of ministries in which to practice. Both of these gifts invite and provoke us to become something new, something more in Christ than we already are; both of them support and challenge our ongoing conversion and make us more fit for God's mission, more up to the divine challenge in each new day.

Fitness for ministry and mission is the result of committed disciplines that make us something new. It may look natural, as if it comes easily to some, but it is always the consequence of hard work and diligent practice. While it was Jesus' divine nature to love, to incarnate God's mission of reconciliation, his earthly ministry came to fullness in part through consistent discipline and practice, as seen in a number of gospel stories like those about his temptation in the desert and his encounter with the persistent mother from Cana.

It is no theological stretch to understand Jesus' change of heart, as recounted in Matthew 15, in terms of the same Identity, Discernment, Practice, and Transformation model we employ in CREDO. In his response to the Canaanite woman, Jesus' self-awareness was challenged, his call to incarnate God's love was further discerned, his practice of compassionate response was extended, all resulting in a transformation that was revealed in his changed response to a persistent woman who did little more than believe in him. In the same way, you and I are continually brought into deeper awareness of our identity as God's beloved, supported by the church and the Holy Spirit in discerning our vocations as Christians, challenged and developed in our varying practices and ministries. We are transformed by the persistent God who believes in us. In this way we become increasingly fit for God's mission.

It is, therefore, important that we choose disciplines that increase our fitness for mission. In our prayer, study, worship, and service, we should seek practices that stretch and strengthen us. Whatever our disciplines, we should see them not as restrictive, but as exercises that develop us physically, spiritually, emotionally, and vocationally—calisthenics that expand our capacity for transformation. It is by that continuing conversion that we become increasingly responsive to God's mission.

One of my disciplines involves walking with light hand weights. I wake up quite early in the morning, and while it is still dark I walk a two-and-a-half mile route through our neighborhood. It stretches my legs and my arms, my circulatory and respiratory systems, and, at that hour, my eyesight. It also stretches me spiritually. It is the time of my most undefended prayer, when the challenges, fears, and hopes of my ministry as a Christian are most exposed to God. It is when I am least shielded from God's response by the convenient distractions of life and work. It is a time of quiet listening, when I am regularly stretched by God in ways that inform how I serve throughout the rest of the day.

Both as individuals and as a church, how fit we are for God's mission, to what degree we are up to the challenges of ministry before us, depends in large part upon the disciplines we practice. The CREDO life-cycle model of identity, discernment, practice, and transformation offers an effective framework for wellness development and provides lifelong calisthenics for our ongoing conversion as the people of God. Use of it (and other disciplines) allows us to flex the muscles, stretch the ligaments, and strengthen the skeletal structures that sustain our ministries and make us increasingly vital and vibrant ministers of the gospel.

Transforming "Growing Pains" into "Identity Gains"[1]

Glen E. Kreiner
Mathew L. Sheep

Integrating being a priest into the whole of my being as a person is what I am working toward. I think I'm there. I'm not there, but I'm moving towards that. That's what takes time.

—◦—

Interviewer: Your attitude about your identity and the priesthood, has that changed over time?

Respondent: Oh yeah, yeah. One way to say is it has dropped from my head to my heart. That's one sort of metaphor. Another is to say that as I was ordained a priest, I put on the vestments and that made me a priest from the outside, in. Then over time, I think this is a maturity in any deep vocation as a teacher, as a physician, as a musician, as an artist. . . . Initially you can be enamored with the image, the symbol, the trappings of the office, the public affirmation. . . . But, if it is a real vocation, it's not from the outside, in, it's from the inside, out. . . . Part of it is going from the doing to the being. It is also sort of from form to content.

Change is constant. But there's no guarantee that the change is good. It's up to us to manage change so that it's positive. As C.S. Lewis once quipped, "It may be hard for an egg to turn into a bird: it would be a jolly sight harder for it to learn to fly while remaining an egg. We are like eggs at present. And you cannot go on indefinitely being just an ordinary, decent egg. We must be hatched or go bad."[2] Thus, how well we grow beyond the "egg" stage and "hatch"—that is, manage changes in terms of our own identity transitions and growth—will determine whether outcomes are beneficial or detrimental, positive or negative.

Our goal in this chapter is to outline three tactics for identity growth that facilitate positive change. While our approach may reflect our academic orientation, we labor in this chapter to provide some very practical ways to think about and "get a grip" on positive identity growth. An individual can use the three tactics we present to improve his or her sense of self in the short- and long-term. The tactics can also be taught—via such activities as counseling, workshops, and sermons.

In this chapter we consider how to focus on a "positive identity." We define a *positive identity* as one that is competent, resilient, authentic, transcendent, and holistically integrated. We define *identity growth* as progressive increases in any or all of these dimensions of positive identity. These dimensions of positive identity, taken together, describe an idealized state of self-concept toward which individuals may strive in a way that is consistent with the assumptions of positive psychology. That is, that benefits derive from a concept of self, focused on developing personal strengths in harmony with one's environment rather than only "fixing" pathologies or weaknesses of the self. Thus, positive identity does not strictly mean the opposite of negative, nor does it connote a "prestigious" identity so much as one that enables the individual to function effectively in the world as an integrated, whole, coherent, competent individual— thereby experiencing greater life satisfaction and happiness.

In the sections to follow, we outline how individuals need not accept their circumstances or rely on good fortune or chance, but rather how they can be proactive in shaping and crafting their identities to develop a more meaningful life. Specifically, we provide details on three tactics that can be used for positive identity growth—developing spiritual identity, transforming identity threats, and experimenting with possible selves.

Developing a Spiritual Identity at Work

It may come as a surprise to some, but psychologists going back to William James[3] have recognized the importance of developing our spiritual identity as a key aspect of the self. Our first tactic thus focuses on the ongoing life process of spiritual identity development, especially in the context of our work and vocation. Such juxtaposition can play a pivotal role in enabling an individual to link the workplace to his/her broader identity growth goals and opportunities.

Four important themes or dimensions to workplace spirituality include: (1) integration of the "whole self" in the context of work; (2) meaningfulness in work; (3) transcendence of self toward a greater whole; and (4) development of one's inner life at work.

The social scientific study of spirituality spans multiple disciplines, but none so related to identity growth as developmental psychology. From this perspective, spiritual identity development is typically defined as

> . . . the process of growing the intrinsic human capacity for self-transcendence, in which the self is embedded in something greater than the self, including the sacred. It is the developmental engine that propels the search for connectedness, meaning, purpose, and contribution. It is shaped both within and outside of religious traditions, beliefs, and practices.[4]

In other words, a sense of "who I am" is shaped by my views of how the world is ordered, of how I approach connections with others, and of what matters most in life. Two mechanisms for positive identity growth from the workplace spirituality literature include holistic integration and transcendence.

First, *holistic integration* can be subdivided into two dimensions, each realized as individuals seek a self-concept progressively marked by (1) identity integration (coherence) and (2) wholeness (completeness). Erikson described the individual quest for identity as a search for "wholeness"—which he defined as "a sound, organic, progressive mutuality between diversified . . . parts."[5] Simply put, we seek to integrate the "parts" of our lives into a coherent whole that makes sense to us. And, while philosophers and theologians have been advocating a coherent identity for centuries, only recently has attention been given to the notion that individuals should be enabled and encouraged to bring all of these "diversified parts"—the "whole self" (cognitive, physical, affective, and spiritual)—into one's work environment.[6] Such integration helps one to infuse work with meaning and purpose in harmony with one's overall beliefs about the meaning and purpose of life. The work environment, rather than fragmenting the self-concept, can thereby become a context in which growth toward a more positive, holistically integrated identity is facilitated. As one of the clergy we interviewed for our "Borders and Bridges" project noted, people "want a consistency between their life and their work. They want something that has a sense of wholeness to them."

The second mechanism is *transcendence* of self-identity. This process begins when individuals view their life's work as "a web of relationships . . . in a larger context that makes it meaningful."[7] Such relationships provide high-quality connections that have been linked both to human growth (more generally) and to the co-construction of valued identities (specifically). When spiritual identity development is viewed as an ongoing quest for transcendence, then the developmental path (growth) toward a *positive* identity proceeds toward an identity that is increasingly self-defined in terms of something greater than oneself—i.e., in terms of a collective, the greater good, a social cause, or the ultimate source of one's beliefs. Paradoxically, loosening the grip on self-interest to embrace larger interests enhances self-concept and the development of a more positive identity. The spiritual dimension of one's identity—marked by internal integration and a connecting transcendence to something greater than oneself—thus functions as a powerful frame within which a positive identity can develop.

Transforming Identity Threats

Sometimes, the fundamental nature of who we are comes into question. This is called an "identity threat." Identity threats can attack your whole self ("Am I really a worthwhile person?") or some particular aspect of your self-concept ("This event suggests that I'm not a good parent."). Identity threats may come in benign forms such as unexpected reactions to a self-initiated job/career transition, or in relatively malignant forms such as job loss, loss of a loved one, or negative feedback from people you respect regarding what you thought was one of your greatest strengths. When our identity is threatened, we have a choice: we can bury our heads and ignore the problem, or we can address it head-on. Research has found that when people recast threats into opportunities, they are more likely to grow from the experience instead of being defeated by it. As people learn from challenging experiences, they develop resilience, which allows them to adapt, cope, and grow despite (or because of) adversity.

More often than not, individuals are primarily concerned with *minimizing threat* rather than *maximizing benefit* from threat. We see minimizing threat as a lost opportunity for growth and therefore suggest a more proactive approach in which an individual can transform an identity threat into an opportunity for growth. To do so, we speak of "identity-threat jujitsu"— a term we coined to invoke imagery of capitalizing on the energy of the threat by transforming it into an opportunity for healthy identity change.

This imagery is similar to the self-defense art of kung fu, in which a person uses the strength of the attacker to leverage the situation instead of receiving the blunt force. Hence, we suggest that people can use the force of the threat strategically as a catalyst for increased self-awareness and positive change. Identity-threat jujitsu can be enacted in at least two ways: (1) reframing identity threats and (2) improving relationships with those individuals that pose threats.

Reframing identity threats. Reframing is the process of transforming the meaning of a stimulus, or looking at something in a new way. Individuals can reframe identity threats by infusing the threat with something of value in order to recast it in a positive light. Individuals can draw upon a gamut of resources for infusing identity threats with positive value, including religious belief systems, occupational or other group-based ideologies, current opportunities, or past successful identity-threat reframing experiences. This represents an opportunity to recast identity threats in generative, positive, and forward-thinking ways.

Improving relationships with individuals that pose threats. In day-to-day interactions and relationships, identity threats can take such forms as negative feedback, stereotypes, or values discrepancies. Often, the response to the identity threat is simple dismissal or denial of the negative information or experience. ("I'll pretend it didn't happen.") Other times, our natural reaction upon identity threat is to condemn the people who attack us or to devalue the source of the identity threat. ("He doesn't know what he's talking about.") The consequence of our labeling others (or their information) as useless often leads to decreasing our contact with or trust in the individual(s) who are the source of the threat. Consequently, we lose out on important insights in the future because we have alienated ourselves from the very people who could provide the most pertinent data in our quest for improvement.

An identity threat often cues the classic "fight or flight syndrome." Either choice has important consequences—choosing "fight" may create an adversarial role with the source of the threat, while choosing "flight" may result in decreased intimacy and closeness with the source of the threat. Either way, the opportunity for growth through challenge is severely diminished or lost entirely. Hence, we suggest that a tactic to use in response to an identity threat is to attempt to *improve* relations with the source of the threat. By engaging with those who are in creative tension with us, we are better able to gain insight into ourselves—the very insight that can encourage identity growth.

Experimenting With Possible Selves

Have you ever thought, "What if I could try being a bit different from how I am right now?" Such a question might be stimulated by curiosity, or it might be a response to a perception that certain aspects of your current identity are not desirable, or that your identity is developing in directions that are not wanted or that are even feared. The tactic of experimenting with possible selves is linked with our first tactic—spiritual identity development—in that one definition of spirituality conceives it as an individual quest for what one considers to be the "sacred" or ultimate.[8] This quest dynamically shapes individual values that may affect how you approach the fundamental question of "Who should I become?"—the driving question that motivates experimenting with possible or provisional selves.[9]

A useful definition of possible selves is: "cognitive components of hopes, fears, goals, and threats" that "function as incentives for future behavior . . . and . . . provide an evaluative and interpretive context for the current view of self."[10] Important elements of that definition include the notion that possible selves are focused on a desirable future identity (as one perceives it) and linked to developing behaviors that will help the individual to attain the future identity. Additionally, possible selves "provide the essential link between the self-concept and motivation."[11] Thus, growth toward a more positive identity is motivated by idealized or aspirational identities toward which one is striving.

Individuals can try out possible selves as a path to positive growth, as well as to take manageable risks through identity experiments. For example, research has confirmed that individuals create a repertoire of possible selves by observing desirable role models (role prototyping) and comparing or contrasting the prototype with themselves (identity matching).[12] In the matching process—and particularly when there is a large gap between one's current identity and that of a hoped-for identity—one is internally motivated to make certain changes that are necessary to grow into the more valued identity. Such changes may also be motivated by something very similar to an identity threat—a perception that a feared possible self (undesirable future identity) is becoming an increasing possibility.[13] In our Borders and Bridges research, an interviewee told us how she had tried different manifestations of her role (e.g., clothing, demeanor, openness) over time to eventually feel more whole as well as more transparent to her parish. The fruits of her labors were shown as she went on to say:

Especially in the community that now knows me, I really can be myself. . . . I think there is a certain playfulness about me that I think in the beginning I probably didn't feel confident being that whole me. I needed to act like more serious or something. I think even as a woman, I'm learning how that makes me a different kind of priest from some of the mentors that I've had. Yeah, I mean, I feel pretty integrated. I think it is a matter of confidence.

Of course, identity matching alone does not in itself bring about a new identity or identity growth. Positive identity growth requires experimentation with new behaviors associated with the desired possible self. This process is carried out by emulating exemplary role models while remaining true to one's self.[14] As one of our interviewees reflected on navigating this tension, he said that earlier in his career he "was trying to go by other people's expectations and the image. As I've discovered, God really calls me to be me." Thus, experimenting with "possible selves" involves being yourself *while* trying something new. It is not a "fake it 'til you make it" strategy for growth. On the contrary, only if the possible self proves to be legitimate and comfortable is it adopted long-term as part of a person's identity.[15]

In addition, a comparison may be made between possible selves and spiritual development. While both are dynamic works in progress, both are ultimately leading toward an integrated or holistic identity. However, because life situations and roles are often in a state of flux, these tactics are always in process. Finally, even though hoped-for possible selves are oriented toward a desired future state, they may have desirable effects in the present. Merely by adopting the future identity as one toward which one is striving may positively impact current behaviors and motivation in such a way as to arouse attitudes of optimism and hope. That is, by thinking of oneself in terms of a desired future state or a more positive identity, an individual develops a more positive outlook so that the psychological capital[16] contributed by that individual to the organization is increased, even though the future identity is a work in progress. This illuminates the linkages between hope and future identities related to possible selves. So, experiment away! Have fun—authentically, of course.

Conclusion

We conclude with a practical caution. The implementation of the three identity-work tactics in this chapter involves transforming an identity pain (problem) into an identity gain (growth). This positive "jujitsu" often requires a good deal of cognitive and emotional energy and, in some cases, no small amount of risk. Ironically, then, these efforts, carried to obsessive extremes, could have an unintended effect of being a stressful series of activities.

Thus, we close with a prescription derived from our interviews with clergy. We asked senior clergy what they would recommend to new priests embarking on their journey of identity growth in their calling. Items of advice most frequently offered were to develop effective social support networks and outside interests—and not to take one's self too seriously. Thus, a balanced approach to positive identity development is marked by diligent effort and contemplative reflection toward an authentic self—while at the same time it is conducted in the spirit of an adventure, even playful experimentation, with potential to realize a competent, resilient, authentic, transcendent, and holistically integrated self.

๑୦๑

Notes

1. This chapter is an adaptation of our previous work, "Growing Pains and Gains: Framing Identity Dynamics as Opportunities for Identity Growth" in, L.M. Roberts and J.E. Dutton, forthcoming, *Exploring Positive Identities and Organizations: Building a Theoretical and Research Foundation.*

2. C.S. Lewis, *Mere Christianity.* (New York: HarperCollins, 2001 edition), 198–199.

3. W. James. *Principles of Psychology: Volumes 1 & 2.* (New York: Holt, 1981/1890).

4. P.L. Benson, E.C. Roehlkepartain, and S.P. Rude. 2003. Spiritual development in childhood and adolescence: Toward a field of inquiry. *Applied Developmental Science* 7: 205–213.

5. E.H. Erikson. *Insight and Responsibility: Lectures on the Ethical Implications of Psychoanalytic Insight* (New York: W. W. Norton & Company, Inc., 1964), 64.

6. While clergy may be more accustomed to this notion because of discernment and ontological shift of the ordination process, the integration of the whole self—including spiritual identity development in its broadest sense—is now being suggested more generally for secular occupations and professions.

7. P.H. Mirvis. 1997. "Soul work" in organizations. *Organization Science* 8:193–206, 199.

8. P.C. Hill and K. Pargament. 2003. Advances in the conceptualization and measurement of religion and spirituality. *American Psychologist 58(1)*: 64–74.

9. H. Ibarra. 1999. Provisional selves: Experimenting with image and identity in professional adaptation. *Administrative Science Quarterly* 44: 764–791.

10. H. Markus and P. Nurius. 1986. Possible selves. *American Psychologist* 41: 954–969.

11. Ibid.

12. Ibarra, 1999.

13. R. H. Hoyle and M.R. Sherrill. 2006. Future orientation in the self-system: Possible selves, self-regulation, and behavior. *Journal of Personality 74:*1673–1696.

14. Ibarra, 1999; Roberts, et al., in press.

15. Ibarra, 1999.

16. F. Luthans, C.M. Youssef, and B.J. Avolio. 2007. Psychological capital: Investing and developing positive organizational behavior. In D. L. Nelson & C. L. Cooper (Eds.), *Positive Organizational Behavior* (Thousand Oaks, CA: Sage), 9–24.

The Alchemy of Effort and Grace
Brian C. Taylor

The Hope of Transformation

I live in New Mexico, and my favorite time of year here is the beginning of fall. It's not just the impossible blue skies, the cool, clear air, the explosive yellow cottonwoods, and the smell of roasting chili. It's the palpable feeling of change. You wake up in the morning and there's something electric in the air, something fresh and new, something that is just starting to become. The world is born again.

This is the same feeling that I sometimes get when returning from a good vacation or retreat. I return to my daily life with hope, with a sense of promise. I see that life is what I make of it, and that it just might be possible to slow down and be "perched a little more lightly on the globe."[1]

Changes such as these are renewing. But if we're paying attention, they also hint at a much more compelling possibility: genuine, deep transformation. This, of course, is the hope that lies at the core of the Christian experience. We die to the old self, as Paul put it, and rise to the new life of grace. Or as the old saying goes, "God loves me as I am, but God loves me too much to let me stay this way." However much we may appreciate our life the way it is, the Christian pilgrimage calls us to change, grow, and ultimately, to be transformed. We not only seek continual maturation in this life, but we believe that it extends into the next, where we shall be transformed "from one degree of glory to another." (2 Corinthians 3:18)

But what are we being transformed *into*? After all, not all change is healthy and good. Some who pursue a religious life transform dramatically, becoming judgmental towards others and increasingly paranoid about the evil world in which they live. Others become obsessed with self-actualization, chasing one spiritual high after another. Both are forms of spiritual change, but they are hardly healthy or holy.

Becoming Christ

In the Christian tradition, we are invited to transform not just generally, but specifically into Christ. We are asked to enter his world, to see with his eyes, to take on his values, to live as he lived. As Paul put it so boldly of those who had died to self and risen in grace, "We have the mind of Christ." (1 Corinthians 2:16) And so we are transformed into a version of Jesus. In Christian transformation, our life becomes characterized, as Jesus' is, by generosity, humility, prophetic fire, forgiveness, trust in God, purity of heart, and unconditional love.

As we are transformed in these ways, we affect others around us, helping the Spirit to build "the kingdom of God," as Jesus called it, so that this world might more resemble the character of Christ. Transformation is not for our own enjoyment; it is so that we can more effectively participate in the redemption of all creation.

Change That Happens to Us

It's fine to talk about these ideals of personal holiness and the transformation of the world, but the real question is *How*? How on earth are we transformed into Christ? How does real and lasting change happen? For we know, as Paul did, how frustratingly insistent our patterns of un-holiness are. "I do not understand my own actions. For I do not as I want, but I do the very thing I hate . . . Wretched man that I am!" (Romans 7:15, 24a) We can have a wonderful experience on retreat or vacation. We can read lofty sentiments such as mine, but when that kid of ours pushes our button for the hundredth time, we explode! When stressful demands at work pile up, our equanimity flies out the window.

One model of transformation relies almost entirely on divine intervention, and it assumes an instantaneous, and sometimes complete, change. This is often how conversion is described: "I was immersed in worldliness, running after women, drugs, and money, living the high life, not even knowing how miserable I was, when BAM! God stopped me cold with a heart attack. I realized that I had been living for nothing. My Christian friend came to see me in the hospital, and there I accepted Christ, and haven't looked back since. I was lost and now am found."

I can't really knock this experience, as long as the new life is actually marked by a Christly character. In fact, it happened to me. In my mid-twenties, I had grown increasingly restless and empty inside, not knowing where my life was headed. Due to a strange series of coincidences within the space of a couple of months, I quickly lost a long-term love, my apartment, my car, my work, even my sense of identity, and was stranded with nowhere to go. The only people who took pity on me and invited me to live with them was a Christian couple who had the odd practice of actually reading the Bible together, praying, and talking openly about their faith. (I had grown up in a staid suburban Episcopal parish.) I asked Christ to live in me, and have never looked back. I was transformed. Now of course, this transformation has had to continue for some thirty years (so far), but it was dramatic and effective when it began.

This is the transformation of Paul on the road to Damascus, knocked off his horse and temporarily blinded. It is the transformation of an alcoholic who one day walks away from a horribly destructive life, into the light of health and sanity. It happens to people because of a crisis, a powerful retreat, or just because we're unconsciously ready for God to slap us upside the head.

Miraculous, transformative intervention either happens or it doesn't. We can't sit around waiting for an epiphany. And yet this doesn't stop some from trying to manufacture one: straining to hear the life-changing voice of God in their heads, saturating themselves with emotional prayer by a crowd of prayer-warriors, or sweating it out in rigorous meditation until enlightenment is attained. When the breakthrough doesn't come, we are disappointed in ourselves (we don't have enough faith) or in God (who apparently doesn't care, or even exist).

Change That We Create

Then there is the kind of transformation that is planned and executed through our own efforts. It comes out of the business model. We see it today in programs to lose weight, get in shape, improve our effectiveness at work, build intimacy in our marriage, and yes, grow spiritually. We set overall goals, identify measurable objectives, and practice the seven steps promoted by the author or workshop leader.

I have not had much experience or success with this model of transformation, but I know that for some it seems to work at least at some levels. They realize that their lives are not going the way they want them to; they get some guidance from someone who can help them organize the chaos of their lives, and they move, step by step, into a new way of being. A rule of life can function this way, as the practitioner gradually takes on a series of activities that he or she knows will bring positive results. My wife essentially did this on a recent vacation, re-plotting her normally distracted week into a format that would allow for quiet time every morning and painting in her studio for two uninterrupted days every week. Previous efforts such as this never worked for her, but this time the timing was right. The plan took hold, and she changed her life for the better.

But the planning/execution model doesn't always work. A well-planned rule of life can become the life-killing law that Paul warned about, a method of measuring our spiritual inadequacy when we fail to keep it perfectly (or worse, a source of smugness when we do). Sometimes we are not ready for change, needing instead to stew awhile longer in our unhappiness in order to learn a lesson at a deeper level. Sometimes we can't see what is best for ourselves, and so any plan we might come up with is worthless. There are times when even if we do know the direction forward, we keep bumping into a familiar roadblock that prevents us from progressing.

A Third Way

When God doesn't seem inclined to slap us upside the head with instantaneous transformation and when we can't transform ourselves through our own efforts alone, there is a third way available to us. It consists of a mysterious interplay of human effort and divine grace.

When I was growing up in California's Bay Area, every self-respecting teenager had to at least try to surf on occasion. What I remember most vividly about my occasional ventures into the surf is not an image of myself standing triumphantly upon the board, riding like King Kamehameha toward the shining sands.

I remember waiting peacefully, bobbing up and down in the water, watching the horizon as swells came in groups, wondering if this set was going to be The One. I remember turning towards shore, paddling hard (the boards were long and heavy in those days), only to fall back when I couldn't catch the momentum of the wave. I remember especially the glorious sensation when my vigorous strokes were magically met by the powerful surge beneath, lifting me up and forward. It was an amazing physical sensation, when, after having waited, discerned, tried, and failed, suddenly my strength and the ocean's strength came together in a glorious alchemy.

So it is with spiritual transformation. We put in our time in prayer, we go to therapy, read books, talk to friends, offer ourselves in worship, and practice our rule of life. We paddle along by our own strength, trying to propel ourselves forward, hoping to catch a wave of freedom, compassion, simplicity, or intimacy with the divine. This is a good and essential part of the spiritual journey. "Work out your own salvation," Paul advised. (Philippians 2:12) Jesus encourages us to "strive first for the kingdom of God," to "strive to enter through the narrow door." (Matthew 6:33; Luke 13:24)

But there is also the waiting on grace. Woven in and out of our striving is another reality: we float in the deep waters, waiting, praying, watching the horizon. Interspersed with our efforts to change is a contemplative dimension, a kind of surrender, a dying to self. This is what Gerald May used to call "creating a little contemplative space" around things, a little breathing room for the Spirit when things are dense. In this contemplative space, we let go of our control, trusting that God is working beneath our understanding and our striving. We float, remaining awake, receptive, watchful.

Eventually the waters beneath us will surge. We receive insight, we hear as if for the first time a familiar passage of scripture, or a part of the old self just sloughs off like dead skin. Our seemingly unfruitful efforts to understand, to change, to move forward are met with an energy beyond ourselves, and we are taken forward.

In this process, effort and grace are not mutually exclusive or even sequential; they are simultaneous, overlapping.

When I was enduring what was, for me, an excruciating process of discernment about whether or not to stand for election as a bishop, I waited in the deep waters of unknowing for months. I prayed every day for guidance. The question was like a cloud, constantly hovering near me. Every time I tried to grab hold of the vapor, my hands would come up empty. Again and again, I had to surrender in faith.

At the very same time, I also made tremendous effort. I studied the history and theology of the episcopate. I talked endlessly to others who were in a position to know the reality of the office. I weighed pros and cons. I did my homework.

One day a good friend who was reading Thomas Friedman's bestseller said offhandedly "Brian, the world *is* flat, you know . . ." Suddenly the waters surged beneath me, and I remembered something I'd always known, but which now became the moment of truth: being a diocesan leader is no higher or bigger or more effective in the kingdom of God than being a good priest, father, husband, friend, and writer. The world is flat. Transformed, I could return to the life I had been given with renewed clarity and passion. This only happened because I had endured a contemplative time that contained, paradoxically, both surrender and effort throughout.

Transformation does not usually happen to us by magic or simply because we will it into being. It happens because we try, we fail, we surrender, we wait, we try again, we get help, we let go, we beat our heads against the wall, we wait some more . . . and all the while, we do our best to trust that the Spirit is actually working harder than we are, beneath the surface of consciousness. Occasionally we catch glimpses of this graceful work, until finally, when the timing is right, it comes out into the open, all of our efforts are matched by the more powerful surge of grace, and we are carried forward.

What was previously impossible for us becomes possible. Our fear drops away like a rusty old ball and chain. We slow down without even having to apply the brakes. Our impulse towards others becomes more consistently patient, more generous. We look in the mirror, and *surprise!* we see the face of Christ.

Over the years, I have learned to trust that if I do my part, the Spirit will go to work as well. I may not be able to see this work for a long time, but as I continue to strive, there is always a part of me that knows God is moving beneath the surface. This enables me to do my part without the corrosive element of fear. I can hold my need for transformation lightly, knowing that in God's good time—in this life and the next—all shall be brought to fulfillment.

Alchemical Experiments

If you are accustomed to either waiting for God's intervention or planning your own self-improvement and you would like to try the alchemy of grace and effort, try one of the following experiments.

1. Pray every day about your need for transformation. Ask only two things: that God will be present and active in this situation; and that you will be shown your obstacles to transformation. Be patient and trust. Something will eventually shift.

2. Practice *Lectio Divina*—a meditative reflection on a short passage of scripture—with a story from one of the gospels. Ask yourself "In this passage, what does Christ ask of me? Can I do this today? If not, how do I need God's grace in order to live in the way I am called to live?"

3. Practice Alcoholics Anonymous' twelve steps to recovery. The first three steps invite us to surrender to grace (admit that our lives are unmanageable, believe that a greater power can restore us, turn our lives over to that power); and the remaining ones require our own effort (moral inventory, willingness to remove shortcomings, make amends, stay in touch with God, carry this message to others and live it daily).

4. If part of your work with other people involves creating change, consider how (or if) you and others:

   a. Make efforts to effect change;
   b. Try to force change when it doesn't come at first;
   c. And/or C. patiently, trustingly, attentively wait until some new breakthrough comes on its own, out of the mix. Try to practice (a) and (c), avoiding (b).

5. Go surfing, skiing, swimming, or kayaking down a river. Do anything that requires that you feel the physical tension between your own efforts and a force greater than you. Feel the interplay between the two. Find your balance. Then apply it to your spiritual life.

☙❧

Note

1. As Peter Levi described monks in *The Frontiers of Paradise: A Study of Monks and Monasteries* (Weidenfeld & Nicolson, 1990).

I Think I Can

Elaine C. Hollensbe

The little train was carrying all these good things to the good little boys and girls on the other side of the mountain. Then all of a sudden she stopped with a jerk. She simply could not go another inch. She tried and she tried, but her wheels would not turn . . . She said "I think I can. I think I can. I think I can." . . . Up, up, up. Faster and faster and faster and faster the little engine climbed until at last they reached the top of the mountain.[1]

All of us can recall times when we faced a challenge at work or in life that raised our thoughts and beliefs about our ability to accomplish it. In fact, obstacles and human responses to them are pervasive in the Bible, novels, movies, and as the opening quote illustrates, even in classic children's stories. Although challenging situations are not rare, responses to them can vary widely. Some people, like the "little engine that could," are able to marshal the confidence and energy they need in the face of challenges. Others feel overwhelmed or paralyzed at precisely the moment when confidence and energy are most needed.

It goes without saying that life often involves changes in attitudes and behavior. In fact, scripture is filled with examples of individuals who have initiated change—Jonah initially denied God's redirection of his life, then changed his attitude toward preaching to the Ninevites, and the faithful son in the parable of the two sons changed his mind and went to work in the vineyard at his father's request. Yet change is sometimes perceived as difficult, if not impossible.

So what causes the divergence in responses to challenge and change? Can confidence beliefs be developed and nurtured, and if so, how? How do these beliefs relate to wellness? In this chapter, I discuss some insights from my own and others' research that can provide a framework for addressing these questions. This chapter is about self-efficacy, or belief in one's ability to engage in a task or change,[2] and readiness to change.

179

Self-Efficacy

> Whether you think that you can or you can't, you're usually right.
> —Henry Ford

> I can do everything through Him who gives me strength.
> (Philippians 4:13, NIV)

Since the late eighties, self-efficacy has received increasing attention from researchers, serving as a study focus across disciplines in the educational, psychological, and organizational sciences.[3] Unlike self-esteem, a global belief that one is a worthwhile person, self-efficacy is a confidence belief that is specific to a task or situation. For example, although I feel that I am a worthwhile person (self-esteem), I feel low confidence in my ability to plan for my retirement (self-efficacy). Therefore, I tend to quickly pitch information I receive in the mail about my retirement and avoid thinking about constructive ways to manage it. Self-efficacy is related to wellness in that low self-efficacy—a perception that demands exceed one's ability to cope—can lead to frustration, anxiety, and stress.[4] More importantly, low self-efficacy beliefs can intensify over time, resulting in a vicious, self-reinforcing downward spiral that leaves a person with an unhealthy and debilitating sense of helplessness.[5] Fortunately, several researchers have also found that self-efficacy is *malleable*, meaning that beliefs about abilities or motivation can be changed by tapping into four "building blocks" of self-efficacy.[6]

Building Self-Efficacy

> If I have the belief that I can do it, I shall surely acquire the
> capacity to do it even if I may not have it at the beginning.
> —Mahatma Gandhi

People form judgments of self-efficacy based on four broad categories of experience.[7] In describing these categories, I include quotes from my research on self-efficacy involving participants in CREDO conferences.[8] I also ask you to reflect on how these "building blocks" might affect your own self-efficacy.

First, *prior experience* is the most potent source of self-efficacy. Self-efficacy beliefs flow from small or large wins experienced while engaging in similar or related tasks in the past. Therefore, reflecting on past accomplishments is one way to build self-efficacy. Note the following comment by a CREDO participant describing a personal insight he discovered by preparing a plan for self-renewal, a process that clearly engaged his self-efficacy:

> I have a lot to offer in a lot of ministries. . . . The thing that gave me
> the most confidence was to go back and look at my achievements in
> ministry. I never bother to look back very often, but looking back
> I realized that in comparison to many of my colleagues, I have done
> a great deal in a pretty short time, and I feel that's pretty positive.[9]

Although reflecting on past accomplishments might appear to be self-centered rather than spiritual, such reflection can improve one's self-efficaciousness and readiness to work on spiritual, physical, financial, or vocational wellness. Thinking about past accomplishments and visualizing successful scenarios can provide positive guides for action.[10]

What prior experiences and accomplishments contribute to your sense of self-efficacy?

Another source of self-efficacy perceptions is *behavior models*. Self-efficacy can be increased by watching others engage successfully in the behaviors that one seeks to accomplish or change. This method of building self-efficacy is well known by company trainers who expose new salespeople to seasoned ones, so the trainees not only learn the ropes of selling, but also to build their efficacy through watching successful sales behaviors.[11] A comment by a CREDO participant demonstrates the importance of role models:

> There were people who were very impressive role models that I
> came across, both as an undergraduate and as a graduate student at
> Yale. There was just something about them. They had something I
> wanted. I just kind of wanted to try on what they were doing.

By identifying and observing a successful role model, one may gain the confidence and the motivation to pursue a desired goal or behavior. Such observations increase one's "can-do" beliefs.

Who are role models for making positive changes in your life?

In addition to these two sources of self-efficacy, *persuasion from others* is another way to build self-efficacy. A pat on the back can go a long way toward increasing a person's belief in his or her ability to handle a situation. Verbal persuasion from a trusted other can give one confidence to try new behaviors and meet challenges head on. For example, the role of trusted others helped to build one priest's self-efficacy to handle a parish crisis:

> [I learned] that I was not afraid to ask for help during the crisis. And asking for help sometimes is not easy for me. So learning that asking for help is really the only way I can get through big challenges, and there's nothing wrong with that, and really there's a lot of grace in that.

Verbal persuasion from others can increase self-efficacy; however, this source is most effective when persuasion comes from people who are trusted, e.g., support groups, friendships, or a spiritual director.

What outlets do you have for receiving verbal persuasion to change?

Finally, a source of self-efficacy perceptions is *assessment of one's physical and emotional* **state**. Self-efficacy can be diminished if a person is emotionally agitated or physically exhausted. People tend to view such physical and emotional signals as evidence that they are not doing well or as "signs of vulnerability and dysfunction."[12] However, being aware of this agitation (rather than continuing to focus steadily on the task or situation at hand) makes it more likely that the agitation can be managed effectively. Here's how one CREDO participant assesses and manages emotional cues she experiences in her parish:

> I'm in a parish that has its struggles and strains, and one of the things I recognized . . . was my ability to both feel and be sensitive to those pains and issues for the parish without feeling sort of anxious for myself personally.

As a person engaging in self-monitoring, she recognizes and acknowledges the sources of her anxiety. Although all of the building blocks of self-efficacy rely on personal agency (through reflective and regulative thought), assessing one's physical and emotional state requires engagement and attention to internal cues that affect confidence beliefs.[13]

What are the physical and emotional states that affect your confidence?

Self-Efficacy and Behavior

To this point, I have identified ways in which self-efficacy can be built and strengthened. Yet, the question remains: Why is it important to do so? The short answer is that self-efficacy has been found to affect a range of behaviors and a host of outcomes including wellness-related ones.[14] Self-efficacy is associated with successful performance on tasks as diverse as career choice, anxiety reduction, addiction control, illness recovery, adjusting to a new job, learning and achievement, adherence to exercise, adaptability to new technology, and stress avoidance.[15] Moreover, research on self-efficacy has shown that its effects even trump ability. That is, if two people have the same ability, the one who has the higher self-efficacy will likely outperform the other.

Self-efficacy beliefs stimulate behavior in at least three ways: through goal-setting processes, responses to failure, and provoking change. First, it is a well-known fact that goals motivate behavior, and people with high self-efficacy tend to set challenging goals, neutralize obstacles, persevere, and learn from setbacks. If a goal is attained, people with a robust sense of self-efficacy set even higher goals. If a goal is not attained, self-efficacious people tend to increase their effort rather than reacting with apathy or despondency.[16] Second, while some self-doubt naturally arises in response to failure, people with high self-efficacy quickly recover and demonstrate resiliency.[17] Highly efficacious people ascribe failures to insufficient effort, while those with low self-efficacy view their failures as caused by low ability.[18] People with low self-efficacy also tend to attribute their successes to things outside of themselves rather than to their own capabilities.

A third way in which self-efficacy beliefs affect behavior is through supporting desired change. People with high self-efficacy are more apt to embrace change, while those with low self-efficacy tend to resist change that they believe will exceed their capacity to cope.[19] Highly efficacious people are more motivated to learn and more motivated to transfer what they have learned into everyday practice and use. In other words, "can-do" beliefs clearly lead to "will-do" behaviors toward personal change. To fully capitalize on self-efficacy effects, however, one must also be ready to change.

Readiness to Change

I think that I do have within me the ability to make plans and to do things differently and to see things differently; that I don't have to just stay stuck in the same patterns. (CREDO participant)

I am about to do a new thing; now it springs forth, do you not perceive it? (Isaiah 43:19)

Readiness to change is determined by people's belief about whether or not changes are needed, as well as by belief in their capacity to successfully make those changes (i.e., self-efficacy). It is "a state of mind about the need for change," an acceptance that change is both necessary and reasonable, and an intention and commitment to pursue change. The probability that changes to improve wellness can be made are enhanced by a person's readiness to change. Low readiness to change can lead to low motivation and even active resistance.[20] Readiness for change is more than just understanding and believing in the change, but also involves developing specific intentions to engage in change.[21]

Much of the research on readiness to change has been published in health-related literature, with a primary focus on curtailing wellness-threatening habits (such as smoking and drugs) and developing healthier ones (such as weight management, a nutritious diet, and use of sunscreen).[22] One popular model—the transtheoretical change model—describes the change process as dynamic involving a series of stages over time.[23] This model is discussed in the next section.

Readiness to Change: A Cyclic, Stage-Based Process

But you are a chosen people, a royal priesthood, a holy nation, a people belonging to God, that you may declare the praises of him who called you out of darkness into his wonderful light. (1 Peter 2:9, NIV)

Readiness to change can be identified by asking people to consider where they are in terms of addressing and changing lifestyle factors that put their wellness at risk. The five stages in which people find themselves include precontemplation, contemplation, preparation, action, and maintenance.[24]

In the *precontemplation* stage, people deny the existence of a wellness problem, minimize it, or attribute it to someone else; at this stage, they are unwilling to change. *Contemplation* is the stage in which people recognize that a wellness opportunity exists and contemplate pursuing it; however, they are not yet taking action toward actually changing their behavior. In the *preparation*, stage people think more clearly about what they can do to improve their wellness and reduce lifestyle factors that jeopardize it. They become committed to change and begin to take concrete "baby-steps" to improve their wellness. At this stage, individuals not only engage in monitoring their wellness, but also seek out information and role models to assist them in making changes.

During the *action* stage, individuals are focused on making a behavioral change, and they take active steps to modify their behavior and the environment to achieve their wellness goals. In this stage, there is an emphasis on skill building, implementing plans, and adjusting the environment to support changes that enhance wellness. Finally, *maintenance* is the stage in which people monitor themselves to ensure that they do not resume unhealthy behavior. In this stage, they acknowledge the effort they have invested in the changes they have made, are sensitive to factors that might lead to recurrence of old habits and behaviors, and adopt strategies to thwart relapse. Depending on the particular wellness change being undertaken, the duration of the maintenance stage may be lengthy and even ongoing.

Getting Ready to Change

And [Jesus] said: "I tell you the truth, unless you change and become like little children, you will never enter the kingdom of heaven." (Matthew 18:3, NIV)

Perhaps the most certain sign of wellness in its broadest sense is . . . readiness to change. It addresses not only past and current conditions but shows how one is progressing toward the future with strong hope that the desired outcomes can be achieved.[25]

Progress through the change stages is "cyclic" and nonlinear in the sense that people move backward and forward through the stages, and may cycle through several times before they achieve the change they desire. According to the model, change is not made quickly or easily; patience and persistence are required. Since the earliest precontemplative stage of change often involves denial, "unfreezing" of existing attitudes, beliefs, and habits is necessary before attempting to implement change. This unfreezing process involves unlearning what one "knows" to be true about oneself and honest evaluation of information about oneself so that potential areas of change can be identified. An exploration of values and personal goals, and identification of reasons for desired change is needed; also, emotions regarding potential change must be experienced and expressed.[26] Once a change has been made, a "refreezing" process is needed to make the changed behavior normal and habitual.[27]

Although readiness to change is an individually held belief, it can be strengthened greatly by a supportive environment. Thus, when trying to understand and increase readiness to change, it is important to consider not only one's beliefs, attitudes, and intentions, but also the context in which changes are being made.

Do you have relationships that support the change you desire? Do you have the spiritual resources you need to make a change?

Wellness Implications of Self-Efficacy and Readiness to Change

Research on self-efficacy and readiness to change points to concrete reasons why investing effort in building these important beliefs can help people become and stay well. Perceptions of low self-efficacy to fulfill desired wellness goals can lead to frustration, stress, and anxiety. When this lack of efficacy involves social relationships, it can also cause depression. A person with low self-efficacy tends to avoid cultivating relationships that could provide satisfaction and buffer the effects of work and life stress.[28] Beliefs about one's ability and readiness to change then are important precursors to behaviors that can lead to wellness. "Can-do" beliefs about oneself and one's ability to change provide the fuel to help individuals transform their wellness goals into lasting accomplishments—to move from "I think I can" to "I knew I could."

. . . Up, up, up. Faster and faster and faster and faster the little engine climbed until at last they reached the top of the mountain.

ॐ

Notes

1. Watty Piper, *The Little Engine that Could*. Illustrated by Lois Lenski (The Platt & Monk Co, Inc., 1930).

2. A. Bandura, *Social Foundations of Thought and Action: A Social Cognitive Theory* (Englewood Cliffs, N.J.: Prentice-Hall; *Self-Efficacy: The Exercise of Control* (New York: W.H. Freeman, 1997).

3. M.E. Gist. 1987. Self-efficacy: implications for organizational behavior and human resource management. *Academy of Management Review* 12:472–485; Scherbaum, C.A., Y. Cohen-Charash, M.J. Kern. 2006. Measuring general self-efficacy. *Educational and Psychological Measurement* 66:1047–1063.

4. S.M. Jex and D.M. Gudanowski. 1992. Efficacy beliefs and work stress. An exploratory study. *Journal of Organizational Behavior* 13:509–517.

5. M.J. Martinko and W.L. Gardner. 1982. Learned helplessness: An alternative explanation for performance deficits. *Academy of Management Review* 7:195–204.

6. M.E. Gist and T. R. Mitchell. 1992. Self-efficacy: A theoretical analysis of its determinants and malleability. *Academy of Management Review* 17:183–211.

7. See note 2 above.

8. For the past ten years I have served as an evaluator/researcher for CREDO conferences. As part of their conference experience, participants completed questionnaires designed to measure self-efficacy in the four conference component areas—financial, physical, vocational, and spiritual—as well as support self-efficacy.

9. Except where indicated otherwise, the quotations included in this chapter are drawn from evaluation data I obtained during a periodic research review of participants in wellness conferences facilitated by CREDO Institute, Inc.

10. A. Bandura. 1989. Human agency in social cognitive theory. *American Psychologist* 44:1175–1184.

11. C.E. Schwoerer, D.R., May, E.C. Hollensbe, and J. Mencl. 2005. General and specific self-efficacy in the context of a training intervention to enhance performance expectancy. *Human Resource Development Quarterly* 16(1):111–129.

12. A.D. Stajkovic and F. Luthans. 2003. Social cognitive theory and self-efficacy: Implications for motivation theory and practice. In L.W. Porter, G.A., Bigley, and R.M. Steers (Eds.), *Motivation and Work Behavior* (New York: McGraw-Hill/Irwin.)

13. See note 9 above.

14. See note 6 above.

15. This sampling of outcomes associated with high self-efficacy is drawn from the following literature sources: R.W. Lent, S.D. Brown, and K.C. Larkin. 1987. Comparison of three theoretically derived variables in predicting career and academic behavior: Self-efficacy, interest congruence, and consequence thinking. *Journal of Counseling Psychology* 34:293–298; T.N. Bauer, T. Bodner, B. Erdogan, D.M. Truxillo, and J.S. Tucker. 2007. Newcomer adjustment during organizational socialization: A meta-analytic review of antecedents, outcomes, and methods. *Journal of Applied Psychology* 3:707–721; R.E. Woodand, E.A. Locke. 1987. The relation of self-efficacy and grade goals to academic performance. *Educational and Psychological Measurement* 47:1013–1024; J.A. Millen and S.R. Bray. 2008. Self-efficacy and adherence to exercise during and as a follow-up to cardiac rehabilitation. *Journal of Applied Social Psychology* 38:2072–2087; T. Hill, N.D. Smith, and M.F. Mann. 1987. Role of efficacy expectations in predicting the decision to use advanced technologies. *Journal of Applied*

Psychology 72:307–314; S.A. Stumpf, A.P. Brief, and K. Hartman. 1987. Self-efficacy expectations and coping with career-related events. *Journal of Vocational Behavior* 31:91–108.

16. R.E. Wood, and E.A. Locke. 1987. The relation of self-efficacy and grade goals to academic performance. *Educational and Psychological Measurement* 47:1013–1024.

17. See note 9 above.

18. A. Bandura. 1991. Social cognitive theory of self-regulation. *Organizational Behavior and Human Decision Processes* 50:248–287.

19. C.E Cunningham, C.A. Woodward, H.S. Shannon, J. MacIntosh, B. Lendrum, D. Rosenbloom, and J. Brown. 2002. Readiness for organizational change: A longitudinal study of workplace, psychological and behavioural correlates. *Journal of Occupational & Organizational Psychology* 75:377–392.

20. T.E. Backer. 1995. Assessing and enhancing readiness for change: Implications for technology transfer. In T.E. Backer, S.L. David, and G. Soucy (Eds.), *Reviewing the Behavioral Science Knowledge Base on Technology Transfer* (Rockville, MD: National Institute on Drug Abuse) 22–24.

21. J. Bernerth. 2004. Expanding our understanding of the change message. *Human Resource Development Review* 3:36–52.

22. S.R. Madsen, D. Miller, and C.R. John. 2005. Readiness for organizational change: Do organizational commitment and social relationships in the workplace make a difference? *Human Resource Development Quarterly* 16:213–233.

23. J.O. Prochaska and C.C. DiClemente. 1984. *The Transtheoretical Approach: Crossing Traditional Boundaries of Therapy* (Homewood, IL: Dow Jones-Irwin).

24. J.O. Prochaska, W.F. Velicer, J.S. Rossi, M.G. Godstein, B. H. Marcus, W. Rakowski, et al. 1994. Stages of change and decisional balance for twelve problem behaviors. *Health Psychology* 13:39–46.

25. CREDO Institute, Inc. 2006. *Episcopal Clergy Wellness: A Report to the Church on the State of Clergy Wellness.*

26. J.V. Petrocelli. 2002. Processes and stages of change: Counseling with the transtheoretial model of change. *Journal of Counseling & Development* 80:22–30.

27. K. Lewin, *Field Theory In Social Science*. (New York: Harper & Row, 1951).

28. C.K. Holahan, and C.J. Holahan. 1987. Self-efficacy, social support, and depression in aging: A longitudinal analysis. *Journal of Gerontology* 42:65–68.

Invitation to a Soul-Fishing Tournament

Barton T. Jones

I love fishing. When I was a young boy I was an enthusiastic worm fisher-man. I was also a cradle Episcopalian. Worm fishing was messy. Church going was very orderly. Permission to be messy was welcome for a small boy like me. After all, I had to go to church every Sunday, dressed 1950s style for the part. Being able to revel in the elemental slime of worms and fish was a relief from the constant pressure to grow up and be orderly and having to sit still in church, especially during long Holy Communion services.

I have fond memories of summers fishing with my grandfather in brushy ponds in the Smoky Mountains of North Carolina. My grandfather was a kind, wiry man of medium height but somewhat taciturn. My younger two brothers and three sisters and I called him "Pop." He sold men's clothing in a large department store in downtown Asheville. Pop and I hunted for night crawlers together on the lawn at night with a flashlight. Then in the early morning we crept through the reeds by ponds to keep from spooking the bass and sunnies and, most importantly, to avoid detection by game wardens. Pop believed that fishing was a God-given right and you shouldn't have to pay some government bureaucrat for a license to pursue it.

Over the many years since then, I did become an avid fly fisherman. I also started working for the Episcopal Church as general counsel to their pension fund about four years prior to the invitation to attend CREDO. Before that, I had worked as a lawyer on Wall Street for twenty-eight years.

Three years ago I came very close to turning down the invitation to attend a CREDO wellness program. I thought of it as an invitation to a "soul-fishing tournament" with accomplished professionals. I am a lay employee in the Episcopal Church and understood that CREDO, at that time, was primarily designed for the clergy of the Episcopal Church. I also remembered soul-fishing once before in my life a long time ago and hated it. Working for the church hadn't changed my attitude at all.

It wasn't because I didn't like fishing or didn't catch anything.

I figured that I had been invited to the CREDO week because I was thought by my colleagues to be a natural soul-fisherman (whatever that looks like) even though I wasn't a priest. After all, I worked for the church and was president of the Anglers' Club of New York, a venerable fly-fishing institution. But appearances can be deceptive and, for me, protective. Yet I didn't know how to respond to the CREDO invitation and still protect my deep dark secret. I hated soul-fishing.

As a young boy, I remember soul-fishing with my father. That could be a stormy experience. His strong, paternalistic discipline frightened me and my naïve attraction to God and my young soul. He made sure we all got to church on time and he didn't spoil us by sparing the rod. Looking back, I could imagine at least one trip with him when I hooked what I thought was my soul and hauled it to the boat. But my father thought it was too ugly and small to be worth keeping. So I threw it back in disgust. That was the last time I ever fished for my soul. I had convinced myself that it would be no fun to catch something so ugly even if it were to become bigger. By the time I left home for college, I managed to put soul-fishing completely out of my consciousness.

In fact the only time I went to church or prayed was for church business, weddings, or funerals. I even joined Grace Church in New York and pledged, in part, so I wouldn't have to get into some song and dance when asked about what church I attended. My job for the church put me in the middle of people who would inevitably ask: "Where's your parish?" I did have a fondness for Grace Church as our three sons went to grammar school there and they held memorable Thanksgiving, Christmas, and graduation services in the main church. But three years after joining that church, the only service I attended was my son Philip's memorial service after he died at age twenty-four in a climbing accident in Yosemite National Park.

I also knew that other participants in the CREDO conference were going to be professional soul-fishing guides—ordained priests. I felt that there was no way I could fake soul-fishing with them. Not only would each of them have landed their own souls—big and beautiful—but they actually helped others fish for souls.

When I got the invitation to CREDO, I felt trapped by circumstances of my own design. If I said no to this invitation, I would reveal right away that awful truth about me—I was not a soul-fisherman. But as an employee of the church I felt compelled to accept the invitation and worry about the risk of exposure later.

As I boarded the plane for the CREDO conference in Memphis, I felt like I did when I was nine years old and my mother drove my brother and me to Eagle's Nest, an Episcopal camp on the Delaware River. We cried the whole way. I had been perfectly happy in the summers running free in neighborhood backyards in New Jersey or on the beaches of Chappaquid-dick Island. "Why was it necessary to take me to a strict church camp?" I whined. Those thoughts morphed into memories of my anxiety about leaving for Army ROTC boot camp at Fort Benning and Fort Bragg during the Vietnam War era. I was not a happy camper then either.

I had completed the pre-conference assessment required for attendance at CREDO. I was okay with the financial, vocational, and health parts, although I was apprehensive about an elevated PSA and possible prostate cancer reported after my physical. Getting treatment for cancer would lead to a whole other experience, like the one I had when I was thirteen and broke both legs at the same time skiing. But I was most apprehensive about my spiritual assessment. I had stopped going to church and didn't pray much. About the best I could say was that I believed that each of us has a spirit and that a higher spiritual force existed. I also knew that I was very dissatisfied with my spiritual state of being.

At CREDO I was assigned to a small group consisting of a retired Episcopal priest, an Episcopal priest who taught at a seminary, and a Presbyterian minister who led a large congregation on the West Coast. Small groups, I was told, would facilitate reflections on the CREDO experience. I felt even more apprehensive now that I would be with only priests. I told my group, when we first met, that there had been an obvious mistake in placing a near heathen like myself with spiritual masters like them. They tried to reassure me that they were also mere mortals. By the end of the week I felt like I was with a group of fishing buddies at a camp on an Alaskan riverbank. We could even relax together, drink beer, and swap stories.

CREDO had evening worship services and one-on-one spiritual counseling sessions. I went along with these, but had to steel myself against the intrusion of unsettling childhood church and family memories. Along the way I rediscovered a sense of spiritual community in those services. I even found myself secretly praying for strength against possible prostate cancer at a healing service.

The counseling sessions introduced me to the idea of finding a spiritual counselor. Like many New York City dwellers, I was familiar with psychotherapy and had spent many hours exploring emotional terrain with a shrink. So I don't know why it hadn't occurred to me that spiritual exploration could occur in a similar way outside the four walls of a church. As the week progressed I could feel myself gradually shedding my defensive armor against serious spiritual exploration.

To my great surprise, after my week at CREDO I ended up thanking my colleague who had extended the invitation to what, for me, had been the prospect of a frightening camping trip. I thanked him because I learned that soul-fishing could be a lot like bone fishing, a kind of fishing that I relish.

Bonefish live around the mangrove swamps in the tropics. You stalk them like you would wild deer in a forest. They are hard to spot. To detect them you have to wear polarized dark glasses and find a moving light-grey shadow in a few feet of water against a mottled sandy bottom. Bonefish spook easily and when disturbed move off like silver torpedoes. If you cast too close to them they bolt.

Bonefish take a fly very delicately. Pull too soon and the fish won't have a chance to bite the fly. Even after they have taken a fly, you have to set the hook ever so gently and immediately let go of your line. If you try to set the hook by hauling back with your rod like you do for salmon or striped bass, a bonefish will instantly snap off the line.

You also really need a guide to catch bonefish. The untrained eye of a novice bone fisherman sees only water and reflections and strains in vain to find a picture-perfect fish emerge from the watery chaos.

Bonefish guides can seem just as intimidating as some priests. They already know how to find the fish. But they can't do much to help you spot the same fish their experienced eyes see. You just have to follow your guide's urgent instructions to cast in a certain direction at a given distance to bonefish you can't see. If you aren't quick and fail to follow the guide's commands exactly, you have no chance of catching that hidden bonefish. Miss a big one and the guides can be vocally critical. This disdain can be very painful to any self-respecting fly-fisherman.

Once you successfully hook a bonefish, you immediately understand why people go to so much trouble to catch one. Bonefish make the fly reel scream and take your fly line to the backing, not just once but several times. You become one with the bonefish in their azure blue water and sparkling white sand flats among the mangroves under a brilliant sun. You are absorbed by nature in an electrifying way.

I discovered at CREDO that I needed a soul-fishing guide to help me work on my technique—why should that be surprising to an experienced bone fisherman! That means learning how to cast close enough to my soul to get its attention but not so close that I spook it. I now know that I have to be very sensitive to spot my soul and detect a bite. Once I sense that I have hooked my soul, I will have to let go until I can begin to bear the full weight of it.

The guides for the CREDO week were definitely experienced. They had guided all types in the spiritual art of soul-fishing. Thanks to them, I felt like I saw the fleeting shadow of my soul for the first time since I threw it back as a boy. I also found out that I already had all the soul-fishing gear I needed. No need to spend a lot of money on new stuff. I didn't need special Jesus lenses. The CREDO guides taught me enough to make soul-fishing engaging again and maybe even an adventure rather than a terrifying trip.

My next goal is to cast close enough to my soul to get a hook up. I know it will take a guide and many more trips before I can do that and, in fact, I may never land it. I just hope I haven't turned into an Ahab, doomed to pursue my Moby Dick. There should be joy in my quest, not only fear and apprehension.

Now I had a very different concern on the way home from the CREDO trip. What would my wife think when I told her about my new enthusiasm for soul-fishing?

We are both spiritual and believe in a greater meaning in life beyond our own existence. But she is just as skeptical as I am when it comes to matters of organized church as a prerequisite for a relationship with God. How would I respond if she said: "Good luck soul-fishing! Sounds like a futile snipe egg hunt to me."

I prepared a tentative answer. I would start soul-fishing again because I had rediscovered on the CREDO trip that I had a soul worth catching. If I could catch my soul, I would be able to connect to my essence and then, hopefully, to the universe and maybe even God. Only then would I become truly connected to all that surrounds me and to all those I love— most importantly to my family, Debby, our sons Peter and Stuart, and our late son Philip.

I have been working with a soul-fishing guide for the three years since I accepted that CREDO invitation. I am still searching and making casts to the fleeting shadow of my soul. At least I have spotted something moving and gained confidence that it is the motion of my soul. I am grateful for reconnecting with fishing in the waters that surround my soul.